The
Mini Crock Pot
Cookbook

Effortless Recipes for One-Pot Delights and
Small Appliance Magic

Jimmie M. Chau

TABLE OF CONTENT

INTRODUCTION

Welcome to The Mini Crock Pot Cookbook! In the fast-paced world we live in, finding time to prepare delicious, home-cooked meals can often feel like a daunting task. But fear not! With the help of your trusty mini crock pot, you can effortlessly create mouthwatering dishes that will tantalize your taste buds and simplify your cooking routine.

In this cookbook, author Jimmie M. Chau presents a collection of 100 delectable recipes designed specifically for your mini crock pot. From hearty breakfasts to savory appetizers, comforting soups and stews to satisfying main dishes, this cookbook covers a wide range of culinary delights to suit every palate and occasion.

The beauty of cooking with a mini crock pot lies in its simplicity and convenience. With just a few ingredients and minimal prep time, you can set it and forget it, allowing the flavors to develop and meld together while you go about your day. Whether you're a busy professional, a student on-the-go, or simply someone who loves good food without the fuss, the recipes in this book are sure to inspire and delight.

Discover the magic of one-pot cooking as you explore the diverse array of recipes that make the most of your mini crock pot's capabilities. From hearty soups and stews that warm you from the inside out to tantalizing appetizers and snacks perfect for entertaining, each recipe is crafted to bring out the best in your small appliance.

Whether you're cooking for yourself, your family, or a gathering of friends, The Mini Crock Pot Cookbook has something for everyone. So dust off your mini crock pot, roll up your sleeves, and get ready to embark on a culinary adventure filled with effortless recipes and unforgettable flavors. Happy cooking!

WHAT IS A MINI CROCK POT?

The traditional slow cooker or crock pot is bigger than a mini crock pot, which is also called a mini slow cooker. It works the same way as the bigger one, but it's made to cook smaller amounts of food.

Most mini crock pots can hold between 1 and 3 quarts of food. This makes them perfect for cooking meals for one or two people or making snacks and dips for parties and other events. They usually have the same basic parts as regular crock pots, like a heating element, a base with temperature controls, and a ceramic or stoneware insert that can be taken out.

These small appliances make slow cooking easy without taking up as much space on the counter or in the cabinet as bigger ones. Families and individuals who want to enjoy the benefits of slow cooking but only need to make a little food at a time like to use them. Mini crock pots are useful because they can cook many different foods, like soups, stews, casseroles, and desserts.

HOW CROCK POT WORKS?

A crock pot, which is also called a slow cooker, cooks food slowly and evenly by using low, steady heat for a long time. In general, this is how it works:

Heating Element: There is a heating element under the cooking pot in the crock pot. The heat that is needed to cook the food comes from this element.

Stoneware or ceramic insert: The cooking pot, which is usually made of stoneware or ceramic insert, is where the ingredients go. When you put this inside the crock pot, that's where the cooking happens.

Lid: The crock pot comes with a lid that fits just right on top of the pot. The lid keeps heat and moisture inside for slow cooking so the food doesn't dry out.

Controlling the Temperature: Most modern crock pots have temperature settings that can be changed so that users can pick from low, high, and sometimes even medium heat. The rate at which these settings set the food cooks.

The ingredients are put into the cooking pot, and the lid is secured. Then, the crock pot is turned on to the chosen temperature setting. The heating element gives heat to the ceramic or stoneware insert as it warms up. This cooks the food slowly.

Slow Cooking: Most cooking methods use higher temperatures for shorter amounts of time. Crock pots, on the other hand, cook food slowly over a number of hours. Slow cooking lets the flavors develop, the meats get tender, and the ingredients mix, making rich and flavorful dishes.

Even Heat Distribution: The crock pot's design makes sure that heat is spread evenly throughout the cooking pot. This keeps the food from cooking unevenly and stops hot spots.

Long Cooking Times: Food can be cooked in a crock pot for several hours or even overnight, depending on the recipe and the finish you want. Because they cook for a longer time, crock pots are great for busy people or families who want to make meals ahead of time with little hands-on time.

Overall, the crock pot is a quick and easy way to make a lot of different foods, from soups and stews to roasts and casseroles, with little work and lots of flavor.

BENEFITS OF MINI CROCK POT?

Mini crock pots are useful in any kitchen, but they're especially useful for people who live alone or in small homes because they have many uses. Many good things come from this:

Perfect Portions: Mini crock pots are made to cook smaller amounts of food, which makes them perfect for single people, couples, or small families. With them, you can make just the right amount of food and not worry about throwing away the extra.

Mini crock pots are very easy to use and are very convenient. You can set it and forget about it after adding the ingredients. You don't have to keep an eye on the food while it's cooking, so you can go about your day without worrying about it.

Versatility: Mini crock pots are very flexible, even though small. A lot of different foods can be cooked in them, like soups, stews, casseroles, dips, appetizers, and even desserts.

Eco-friendly: Because they cook less food and have smaller heating elements, mini crock pots usually use less energy than larger slow cookers. In the long run, this could help you save money on your energy bills.

Planning meals: Mini crock pots are great for planning meals and cooking a lot at once. Make meals ahead of time and freeze them in single servings, ready to reheat whenever you need them. This can save you time during the busy workweek, and make sure you always have a tasty home-cooked meal on hand.

Portable: Many mini crock pots have lids that lock and stay on, making them easy to move around. They are great for potlucks, picnics, football games, and other events where you want to share a warm dish.

Easy to Clean: Most mini crock pots are simple to clean because they have stoneware inserts that can be taken out and washed by hand or in the dishwasher. This makes cleaning up easy, which saves you time and work after eating.

In general, mini crock pots are smaller and easier to use than regular slow cookers, but they still do all the same great things. These appliances are very useful because they let you make tasty home-cooked meals with little trouble, whether you're cooking for one person or a small group.

TIPS AND TRICKS FOR USING CROCK POT?

A crock pot, which is also called a slow cooker, can make cooking meals easier and taste better. To get the most out of your crock pot, here are some tips and tricks:

Pick the Right Size: Make sure the size of the crock pot is right for the food you're cooking. If you fill the crock pot too much or too little, it can change the cooking time and results.

Before you use them, prepare the ingredients. This will save you time in the morning or before a busy day. You can quickly assemble your dish in the morning if you chop the vegetables, trim the meat, and measure the spices.

Correctly Layering Ingredients: Put ingredients in the crock pot in layers based on how long they take to cook and how dense they are. Root vegetables and heavy meats should go at the bottom of the pan. Lighter foods and liquids should go on top.

Use Less Liquid: Because slow cookers keep the moisture in, you usually need less liquid than when cooking the old-fashioned way. It's better to start with less liquid than you think you'll need because too much liquid can make the dish too watery. If you need to, you can always add more liquid later.

Pack only a little in the crock pot. Leave some space around the edges so that air can flow and cooking is even. When fewer people are in a kitchen, food may cook evenly and take longer.

Don't Peek: Don't open the lid; check on your food often. Each time you lift the lid, heat is lost, which makes the food take longer to cook. Don't take the lid off until it's time. Trust the slow cooking process.

Change the Seasonings: As the food cooks slowly, the flavors can blend and soften, so make the necessary changes to the seasonings and spices. Add more seasoning near the end of the cooking time to get the desired taste.

Tough Cuts of Meat: Chuck roast and pork shoulder are two tough cuts of meat that do best when cooked slowly. Collagen and connective tissue are broken down by the low, slow heat, which makes the meat tender and flavorful.

Thicken Sauces at the End: If your dish still has too much liquid after cooking for a long time, you can thicken the sauces by adding a slurry of cornstarch and water to the crock pot. Let it cook on high for another 15 to 30 minutes or until it gets thicker.

Easy to Clean Up: Use slow cooker liners or spray cooking spray on the insert before adding the food to make cleanup easier. After cooking is done, let the crock pot cool down before using warm, soapy water to clean it or putting the insert that can be taken out in the dishwasher.

These tips and tricks will help you get good at slow cooking so you can use your crock pot to make tasty meals without much trouble. Try out various cooking methods and recipes to find your favorite foods!

WHAT CAN YOU COOK WITH CROCK POT?

Stews and soups: Crock pots are great for making hearty stews and soups. Slow cooking lets the flavors in soups like chicken noodles, beef stew, and chili develop and blend together beautifully.

Rough cuts of meat, like beef chuck roast or pork shoulder, get soft and flavorful when cooked slowly in a crock pot. To make a full meal, add vegetables and seasonings.

Pulled Pork or Chicken: Slow cooking is the best way to get thick, juicy pulled pork or chicken. Season the meat in the crock pot with your favorite sauce or marinade to make it easy to shred with a fork.

Curries and Casseroles: You can make tasty curries and casseroles in your crock pot. Mix meat, vegetables, spices, and coconut milk or broth together for a warm and fragrant meal.

Recipes for Vegetarians: Crock pots can be used for many things, including making tasty vegetarian meals. Try making vegetable curry, lentil soup, or quinoa-stuffed bell peppers for a healthy and filling meal.

Spreads and snacks: Crock pots are great for parties because they can keep spreads and snacks warm all night. There are a lot of different appetizers that everyone will enjoy, from cheesy dips to meatballs in sauce.

Desserts: Yes, a crock pot can be used to make desserts! The slow cooker can turn plain foods into rich desserts like apple crisps, chocolate lava cake, and bread pudding with just a few simple ingredients.

Breakfast Food: Breakfast foods cooked in the crock pot are a great way to start the day. You can make overnight oats, breakfast casseroles, or even cinnamon rolls ahead of time and have them ready to eat when you wake up.

These are just a few of the many meals that a crock pot can work with. You can do anything if you're creative and willing to try new things.

1. BANANA BREAD

Prep Time: 15 Minutes | Cook Time: 3 Hour

Total Time: 3 Hour 15 Minutes | Serving: 6

Ingredients

- ✓ 1/4 tsp baking soda
- ✓ 1/2 cup of chopped nuts strawberries, or blueberries
- ✓ 1 tsp vanilla
- ✓ 2 tsp baking powder
- ✓ 3/4 cup of light brown sugar
- ✓ 2 eggs well beaten
- ✓ 3 bananas ripe, mashed
- ✓ 1 3/4 cup of all purpose flour or gluten free ap flour mix
- ✓ 1/2 tsp salt
- ✓ 1/3 cup of butter or margarine

Instructions

1. Coat a 3-quart crockpot or a small loaf pan with cooking spray and flour. Then, put it inside a bigger crockpot. Combine the sugar and butter together with a mixer until they are light and fluffy.
2. Eggs, vanilla, and mashed bananas should be added slowly. Mix until it's smooth.
3. Mix flour, baking powder, salt, baking powder, and baking soda in a small bowl by sifting them together. Add the flour mixture slowly while beating the creamed mixture.
4. Add nuts or fruit and mix well. Put it in a slow cooker or a pan.
5. Put the lid on and cook on high for two to three hours. Let the bread cool down, then put it on a platter to serve.

2. STRAWBERRY JAM

Prep Time: 30 Minutes | Cook Time: 1 Minutes

Total Time: 31 Minutes | Serving: 16

Ingredients

- ✓ 2 tbsp corn starch
- ✓ 1/4 cup of water
- ✓ 1 pound strawberries (4-5 cups) quartered
- ✓ 1/4 cup of orange juice (juice of one whole orange, squeezed)
- ✓ 1 cup of sugar

Instructions

1. Strawberry (1 pound, 4 to 5 cups), sugar (1 cup)
2. In the inside pot, mix the strawberries and sugar together. Put them away for at least half an hour. After 30 minutes, if the berries don't have much liquid coming out, stir them and let them sit for another 15 minutes.
3. Mix the berries and the juice that was squeezed out of them together. Put the orange juice in.
4. Close the lid, lock it, and turn off the valve that lets steam out. Set the manual button to high for one minute if you have one. Press Steam and set it to 3 minutes if it doesn't already. Hit "Start" or "Stop." Keep a close eye on the timer. When the display says "2" after one minute, press Start/Stop to end the cooking time.
5. All of this for a full 15-minute natural pressure release. Take off the lid and mash the strawberries with a potato masher until they reach the consistency you want. I like to leave some big strawberry pieces in mine.
6. Press "Start" and then "Brown/Saute." Bring the jam to a low boil.
7. Put cold water and cornstarch in a small jar. Pour it in slowly and stir it around. Let it cook down and get thicker for two to three minutes. To turn off the heat, press Start/Stop. Take out the inner pot and let the jam cool down. Place cooled jam in jars and put them in the fridge.

3. BREAKFAST CASSEROLE

Prep Time: 20 Minutes | Cook Time: 6 Minutes

Total Time: 6 Hour 20 Minutes | Serving: 8

Ingredients

- ✓ 2 green onions sliced
- ✓ ½ tsp black pepper
- ✓ 1 small finely diced white onion about ½ cup
- ✓ 2 cups of sharp cheddar cheese shredded, about 8 ounce
- ✓ 1 pound bacon, sausage, or ham cooked & crumbled or diced
- ✓ 1 green bell pepper diced
- ✓ 1 tsp garlic powder
- ✓ 1 bag frozen hash brown potatoes 32 ounces
- ✓ 1 red bell pepper diced
- ✓ 1 tsp salt
- ✓ 1 ½ tsp dry mustard powder
- ✓ 1 cup of milk
- ✓ 12 eggs

Instructions

1. Cook the bacon or sausage and then break it up. Take out all but 1 tbsp of the fat from the pan.
2. If you want, you can use the fat to soften the onion. This isn't necessary, but it will make the onion taste less sharp.
3. Clean and grease a 6-quart slow cooker. Put half the meat, onions, peppers, cheese, and hash browns in half. Do it again, ending with cheese this time, but don't stir.
4. Stir the eggs, milk, and spices in a medium bowl. Put the egg mixture in the slow cooker and mix it in.
5. Set the timer to low and leave it on for 7 to 8 hours. Take the casserole out of the oven and let it rest for 15 minutes.

4. HOT CHOCOLATE

Prep Time: 5 Minutes | Cook Time: 2 Hour

Total Time: 2 Hour 5 Minutes | Serving: 8

Ingredients

- ✓ 1 cup of half and half cream
- ✓ 1/2 cup of unsweetened cocoa powder
- ✓ 1 cup of mini marshmallows
- ✓ 1/2 cup of semisweet chocolate chips
- ✓ 1 tsp vanilla extract
- ✓ 3/4 cup of granulated sugar
- ✓ 5 cups of whole milk

Instructions

1. Mix the milk, cream, sugar, chocolate chips, and cocoa powder in a saucepan that holds 2.5 to 4 quarts. Apply a whisk to break up the cocoa powder.
2. Heat on low for two hours until the chocolate melts and the hot chocolate is warm all through.
3. Add the vanilla and sprinkle the mini marshmallows on top. Cover the slow cooker and turn it off if you want the marshmallows to get softer. Let it sit for 5 minutes. Do it.

5. BLUEBERRY OVERNIGHT FRENCH TOAST

Prep Time: 10 Minutes | Cook Time: 4 Hour

Total Time: 4 Hour 10 Minutes | Serving: 4

Ingredients

- ✓ 1 tsp vanilla
- ✓ 1/4 cup of melted butter
- ✓ 1 tsp cinnamon
- ✓ 1 cup of lightly packed brown sugar
- ✓ 1 1/2 cup of milk
- ✓ 12 slices bread
- ✓ 1 tsp salt
- ✓ 5 eggs
- ✓ 1 1/2 cup of blueberries, either fresh or frozen

Instructions

1. Cover the slow cooker insert with cooking spray. Add about a third of the brown sugar mixture to the bottom of the insert. Cover all the bread slices with the rest of the spread.
2. Cut or tear half of the bread to fit into the slow cooker, then sprinkle all the blueberries on top. Place the rest of the bread on top in a way that makes it slightly overlap.
3. Add the eggs, milk, vanilla, and salt to a large mixing bowl. Use a whisk to mix the ingredients well. Slowly pour the egg and milk mix over the bread layers, and then press down on the bread to cover it. Put it in the fridge overnight or for at least two hours.
4. Setting the slow cooker to LOW heat for 4 hours is what you need to do when you're ready to cook.
5. Put warm maple syrup on top and add fresh blueberries to the side.

6. VEGETABLE OMELETTE

Prep Time: 15 Minutes | Cook Time: 2 Hour

Total Time: 2 Hour 15 Minutes | Serving: 6

Ingredients

- ✓ 1/2 cup of zucchini
- ✓ 1/4 cup of string beans
- ✓ 8 eggs
- ✓ 1/4 tsp pepper
- ✓ 1/2 cup of carrots
- ✓ 1 tbsp extra virgin olive oil
- ✓ 1/2 cup of potatoes
- ✓ 1/2 tsp salt
- ✓ 1/2 cup of parmesan cheese
- ✓ 1/4 cup of red bell
- ✓ 1 onion

Instructions

1. Get an easy-to-use bowl and add the eggs, Parmesan cheese, salt, and pepper.
2. Put the onions in a saucepan with extra virgin olive oil and cook them over medium heat for two minutes. Then add all the other vegetables. Let it cook for 10 minutes or until it's almost done.
3. Put the vegetables in the slow cooker and put the egg mixture. Make sure the vegetables are well covered. For two hours, set it to high.

7. RICE PUDDING

Prep Time: 10 Minutes | Cook Time: 2 Hour 30 Minutes

Total Time: 2 Hour 40 Minutes | Serving: 4

Ingredients

- ✓ ¾ cup of long-grain white rice
- ✓ 4 cups of milk
- ✓ 1 tsp vanilla extract
- ✓ 1 cinnamon stick
- ✓ 40 g (1.4 ounce) unsalted butter
- ✓ ½ cup of sugar

Instructions

1. First, run cold water over the rice to clean it.
2. Put everything in the slow cooker and stir it around until the sugar is gone.
3. For two and a half to three hours on high, or until the rice is done and the liquid is thick. Serve and enjoy.

8. CINNAMON ROLL CASSEROLE

Prep Time: 15 Minutes | Cook Time: 2 Hour

Total Time: 2 Hour 15 Minutes | Serving: 9

Ingredients

- ✓ 1½ tsp Vanilla
- ✓ 5 Eggs
- ✓ 1 tsp Cinnamon
- ✓ ¾ cup of Milk
- ✓ ¼ cup of Real Maple Syrup
- ✓ 2 (17.5 ounce) tubes Refrigerated Cinnamon Rolls "Grands Size" (with Icing)

Instructions

1. Use cooking spray on the slow cooker crock.
2. Take the cinnamon rolls out of the tubes and cut them in half, but don't cut them in half. Do not use the icing.
3. Put the cinnamon rolls that have been cut in half at the bottom of the slow cooker. They will grow, so don't put too many of them together. Just put them on top of each other so they barely touch. Use the extra to make a second layer.
4. Put the eggs, milk, maple syrup, cinnamon, and vanilla in a bowl. Mix everything together with a whisk. After that, pour it over the cinnamon rolls.
5. Put one of the icing cups of in the microwave for 7-10 seconds to warm it up. Then, drizzle it over the cinnamon rolls.
6. Set the heat to low and let it cook for one to two hours. Keep an eye on it so the bottom doesn't get too brown.
7. Turn off the slow cooker and take off the lid when it's done.
8. Warm up the last cup of icing before you serve the hot cinnamon roll casserole and drizzle it.
9. Put some vanilla ice cream or extra maple syrup on top of a big spoonful (or both!).

9. STICKY BUNS

Prep Time: 10 Minutes | Cook Time: 2 Hour

Total Time: 2 Hour 10 Minutes | Serving: 6

Ingredients

- ✓ 1 tube refrigerated biscuit dough
- ✓ 1 c. Pecan halves
- ✓ 1/2 c. packed brown sugar
- ✓ 1 c. butter, melted (divided)
- ✓ 1/2 c. cinnamon sugar

Instructions

1. Mix ½ cup of butter with brown sugar in a medium bowl. Whisk the mixture until it is smooth. You can put half of the mix in the bottom of a slow cooker. Add about half of the pecans on top of the mix.
2. Pour the cinnamon sugar into a separate shallow bowl and put the rest of the melted butter into the first one. Dip each round of biscuit dough in butter, then coat it in cinnamon sugar. Put cookies on top of the pecans. Cover the biscuit dough with the rest of the butter and brown sugar mixture. Then, add the rest of the pecans on top. After cooking on high heat for about an hour and a half to two hours, the dough will be done.
3. Use a butter knife to go around the sticky buns outside the slow cooker. Carefully flip all the sticky buns onto a serving platter at once. Warm up and serve.

10. CHOCOLATE CHIP SCONES

Prep Time: 5 Minutes | Cook Time: 1 Hour 30 Minutes

Total Time: 1 Hour 35 Minutes | Serving: 8

Ingredients

- ✓ 150 ml milk
- ✓ 100g chocolate chips
- ✓ 30g caster sugar
- ✓ 225g self raising flour
- ✓ 55g butter cubed
- ✓ Pinch of salt

Instructions

1. Put the sugar, salt, and flour and mix them together.
2. Add the butter and rub it in rough. Add the milk and mix it in to make a soft dough. Add the filling or chocolate chips and mix well.
3. Slowly bring it together and shape it into a circle. Use a knife to make lines on the top where you will cut the triangles.
4. Spread out the dough in your slow cooker and add it slowly.
5. Cover and cook on high for about 1.5 hours or until a skewer comes out clean. Place a tea towel under the lid to keep the dough from getting wet.
6. Take it out of the pot, let it cool down, and then cut it into triangles.

12. PEACH CRISP

Prep Time: 15 Minutes | Cook Time: 4 Hour

Total Time: 4 Hour 15 Minutes | Serving: 8

Ingredients

- ✓ 4 cups of sliced peaches
- ✓ ⅓ cup of butter, softened
- ✓ ½ cup of uncooked old-fashioned oats
- ✓ ⅓ cup of brown sugar
- ✓ 1 tsp ground cinnamon
- ✓ nonstick cooking spray
- ✓ ½ cup of all-purpose flour
- ✓ ⅓ cup of white sugar

Instructions

1. Spread cooking spray around the inside of a slow cooker.
2. Mix the flour, oats, butter, brown sugar, white sugar, and cinnamon in a big bowl.
3. Put peaches in the bottom of the slow cooker that has been prepared. Put the flour mix on top of the peaches.
4. On Low, cover and cook for 4-6 hours or until the peaches bubble.

11. MEXICAN BREAKFAST CASSEROLE

Prep Time: 10 Minutes | Cook Time: 3 Hour

Total Time: 3 Hour 10 Minutes | Serving: 8

Ingredients

- ✓ 8 eggs
- ✓ 1 pound bulk sausage, cooked and drained
- ✓ 3/4 cup of sliced green onions
- ✓ 1 Jalapeno, seeded, finely chopped
- ✓ 1/2 cup of salsa, optional
- ✓ Cooking spray
- ✓ 1 1/2 cups of low-fat milk
- ✓ Pickled Jalapeno slices, optional
- ✓ 1 red bell pepper, chopped
- ✓ 9 corn tortillas
- ✓ 2 cups of low-fat Mexican blend cheese

Instructions

1. Use a whisk to stir the eggs, milk, and Jalapeno in a medium-sized bowl. Mix the cheese, chopped red pepper, green onions, Jalapeno, and sausage in a different bowl. Put them both away.
2. Cooking spray should be used on a 5- to 6-quart pot. Tear up three tortillas and put them in a slow cooker. Make sure they cover the bottom.
3. Over half of the sausage, bell pepper, green onion, and cheese mix on top of the tortillas in the slow cooker. Cover with three tortillas, then add the rest of the sausage, vegetable, and cheese mix on top of those tortillas. Add the last three tortillas on top, tearing them as needed to cover the mixture. Cover the tortillas with the egg mix.
4. Put the lid on top and cook on low for 4-5 hours or high for 2-3 hours, or until the center is set 5 and the temperature reaches 160°F. You can top it with salsa, Jalapenos, scallions, or anything else you like.

13. SWEET AND SOUR MEATBALLS

Prep Time: 10 Minutes | Cook Time: 3 Hour 10 Minutes

Total Time: 3 Hour 20 Minutes | Serving: 8

Ingredients

- ✓ 1/2 tsp pepper
- ✓ 1/2 cup of breadcrumbs
- ✓ 1/4 cup of onion finely diced
- ✓ 2 pounds ground beef I use 90% lean
- ✓ 1/2 tsp garlic powder
- ✓ 2 eggs
- ✓ 12 ounce bottle chili sauce
- ✓ 1 tsp salt
- ✓ cooking spra
- ✓ 2 tbsp parsley
- ✓ 1 1/2 cups of grape jelly

Instructions

1. Bring the broiler up to temperature. Put foil around the edges of a sheet pan and spray cooking spray on them.
2. Put the onion, breadcrumbs, ground beef, salt, pepper, and garlic powder in a large bowl. Combine everything completely by stirring.
3. To make meatballs about an inch in diameter from the meat mixture, put them in the pan that has been previously prepared. 8 to 10 minutes under the broiler or until golden brown.
4. Make the sauce while the meatballs are cooling down.
5. Use 30-second increments in the microwave or medium-high heat to melt the grape jelly. Pour in the chili sauce while whisking until the jelly has melted.
6. Utilize cooking spray to cover a slow cooker. After adding the meatballs, pour the sauce on top. Toss it to coat.
7. After 3 hours, turn the heat down to low. After serving, sprinkle with parsley.

14. BBQ CHICKEN SLIDERS

Prep Time: 5 Minutes | Cook Time: 7 Hour

Total Time: 7 Hour 5 Minutes | Serving: 6

Ingredients

- ✓ 20 ounce BBQ sauce
- ✓ 1 pound chicken breast
- ✓ 1 package Hawaiian rolls
- ✓ 2 cups of coleslaw

Instructions

1. Cover the chicken in BBQ sauce and put it in the crock pot.
2. With the lid on, cook on low for 7-8 hours or high for 4 hours.
3. Chicken should be shredded with two forks or a meat shredder, and the sauce should cover all of the chicken.
4. Cut Hawaiian rolls in half and put as much chicken as you want on the bottom of each one.
5. To make a slider sandwich, put the top half of the bun on top and add as much coleslaw or other toppings as you like.
6. Serve and enjoy!

15. LITTLE SMOKIES

Prep Time: 5 Minutes | Cook Time: 2 Hour

Total Time: 2 Hour 5 Minutes | Serving: 12

Ingredients

- ✓ ½ tsp ground cayenne pepper
- ✓ 1 cup of barbecue sauce
- ✓ 28 ounces little smokies sausages
- ✓ 1 tbsp apple cider vinegar
- ✓ ½ cup of grape jelly

Instructions

1. Put the BBQ sauce, grape jelly, apple cider vinegar, and ground cayenne in a bowl and mix them together. Put the smokey bits in the crock pot.
2. Place the little smokies in a bowl and add the sauce. Stir to mix.
3. Turn the heat down to low, cover, and cook for two to three hours or until everything is warm.

16. CORN AND JALAPENO DIP

Prep Time: 10 Minutes | Cook Time: 2 Hour 15 Minutes

Total Time: 2 Hour 25 Minutes | Serving: 6

Ingredients

- ✓ 2 jalapenos, seeded and diced
- ✓ 4 slices bacon, diced
- ✓ ½ cup of sour cream
- ✓ 2 tbsp chopped chives
- ✓ 1 cup of shredded Pepper Jack cheese
- ✓ 3 (15.25-ounces) cans whole kernel corn, drained
- ✓ 8 ounces cream cheese, cubed
- ✓ ¼ cup of grated Parmesan cheese
- ✓ Kosher salt and freshly ground black pepper, to taste

Instructions

1. Set the big pan on medium-high heat. Add the bacon and bake until it is brown and crispy, six to eight minutes later. Place the food on a plate that has been lined with paper towels.
2. In a 6-quart slow cooker, mix the corn, jalapenos, sour cream, Pepper Jack cheese, and Parmesan. Add salt and pepper to taste. Combine everything well by stirring. Put some cream cheese on top.
3. Lower the heat and cover the food. Leave it alone for two hours.
4. Take off the lid and mix the cream cheese in well. Put a lid on top and cook on high heat for 15 more minutes.
5. If you want, you can serve it right away with bacon and chives on top.

17. CHEX MIX

Prep Time: 10 Minutes | Cook Time: 2 Hour | Total Time: 2 Hour 15 Minutes | Serving: 12

Ingredients

- ✓ 3 cups of rice Chex cereal
- ✓ 1 tsp onion salt
- ✓ 1 cup of cashews
- ✓ 3 cups of corn Chex cereal
- ✓ 1 cups of pretzels
- ✓ ¼ cup of Worcestershire sauce
- ✓ 1 cup of pecan halves
- ✓ 1 cup of redskin peanuts
- ✓ 1 tsp onion powder
- ✓ 2 tsp seasoning salt
- ✓ 2 cups of wheat Chex cereal
- ✓ 1 cups of goldfish crackers
- ✓ 1 cup of Cheez-its crackers
- ✓ 1 tsp garlic powder
- ✓ 1½ cup of melted butter

Instructions

1. In the slow cooker, mix the cereal, pretzels, crackers, and nuts together.
2. Seasoning salt, onion powder, garlic powder, and onion salt should all be mixed together with melted butter.
3. Then, pour the butter mixture over the slow-cooked cereal. Toss until everything is well combined.
4. Set the heat to LOW and stir the food every 30 minutes for two hours.
5. Place the mix on parchment paper to cool. After it cools down, put it in containers that won't let air in for up to a week.

18. SPINACH ARTICHOKE DIP

Prep Time: 15 Minutes | Cook Time: 1 Hour | Total Time: 1 Hour 15 Minutes | Serving: 16

Ingredients

- ✓ 1 cup of parmesan cheese shredded
- ✓ 1 cup of sour cream
- ✓ 2 cloves garlic minced, more to taste
- ✓ 12 ounces cream cheese softened
- ✓ 2 cups of mozzarella cheese shredded
- ✓ 16 ounce frozen chopped spinach thawed and squeezed dry
- ✓ 12 ounces marinated artichoke hearts chopped

Instructions

1. Use a hand blender to make the cream cheese, sour cream, and garlic fluffy. Put them all in a large bowl and mix them together.
2. Add the artichokes, spinach, and cheese and mix until everything is well mixed. If you want, you can add more salt after tasting.
3. It can be cooked on high for one hour or low for two hours in a 6-quart crock pot. After that, stir it and let it get warm.

19. SWEET AND SPICY KIELBASA SAUSAGE

Prep Time: 10 Minutes | Cook Time: 6 Hour

Total Time: 6 Hour 10 Minutes | Serving: 8

Ingredients

- ✓ 1 10.5 ounce jar red pepper jelly
- ✓ 2 tbsp honey
- ✓ 3 packages kielbasa approx 40 ounces, cut into 1 inch cubes
- ✓ 2 cups of BBQ sauce
- ✓ 2 tbsp dark brown sugar
- ✓ 1 tbsp red pepper flakes

Instructions

1. Put everything in the slow cooker together. Use a stir to mix.
2. If you want to cook on high for 3.5 to 4 hours, start cooking on low for 6 hours and then raise the heat to high for the last 30 minutes.
3. Every 30 minutes, stir the kielbasa to ensure it doesn't catch fire on the bottom. Enjoy!

20. BUFFALO CHICKEN DIP

Prep Time: 10 Minutes | Cook Time: 2 Hour 10 Minutes

Total Time: 2 Hour 20 Minutes | Serving: 16

Ingredients

- ✓ 2/3 cup of blue cheese crumbles, plus more for topping
- ✓ 8 ounce shredded sharp cheddar cheese
- ✓ 2 packages cream cheese, softened
- ✓ 1 cup of buffalo sauce, plus more for topping
- ✓ 2/3 cup of ranch dressing
- ✓ 8 ounce shredded pepper jack cheese
- ✓ 4 cup of shredded, cooked chicken
- ✓ Chopped chives, for topping
- ✓ Carrots, celery sticks, and tortilla chips, to serve

Instructions

1. Put the chicken, cheddar cheese, pepper jack cheese, cream cheese, buffalo sauce, ranch dressing, and blue cheese in a 6-quart slow cooker. Mix the cheeses together. Cover and cook on low for two to four hours, stirring every now and then.
2. Blue cheese crumbles, buffalo sauce, and chives should be added to the dip before it is served. Keep warm for up to two hours. Carrot sticks, celery, and tortilla chips should go with it.

21. GRAPE JELLY MEATBALLS

Prep Time: 15 Minutes | Cook Time: 3 Hour 25 Minutes

Total Time: 3 Hour 40 Minutes | Serving: 16

Ingredients

Meatballs:

- ✓ 1 large egg
- ✓ 1 pound ground beef
- ✓ ½ tsp black pepper
- ✓ 1 small yellow onion, finely chopped (about ½ cup)
- ✓ ½ cup of (54g) fine dry breadcrumbs
- ✓ 2 tsp kosher salt
- ✓ 2 tbsp flat-leaf parsley, chopped
- ✓ 1 pound ground pork
- ✓ 2 cloves garlic, minced
- ✓ ½ cup of (100g) grated parmesan cheese
- ✓ ½ cup of (122.5g) milk

Sauce:

- ✓ 1 ¼ cups of (12 ounces) grape jelly
- ✓ 1 ¼ cups of (12 ounces) chili sauce

Instructions

1. Warm the oven up to 350°F.
2. Ground beef, pork, beaten egg, cheese, parsley, salt, and pepper should all be mixed in a large bowl. Just mix the two things together.
3. Put the milk, breadcrumbs, garlic, and onion in a medium-sized bowl.
4. When you add milk to the meat mixture, be careful not to mix the ingredients too much.
5. Shape the meat into balls of the size you want, greasing your hands first to keep the meat from sticking, and place them on a baking sheet lined with parchment paper.
6. Put the meat in a hot oven and roast it for about 25 minutes, or until the outside is browned and a meat thermometer hits 165°F.

22. CANDIED SPICED NUTS

Prep Time: 10 Minutes | Cook Time: 3 Hour

Total Time: 3 Hour 10 Minutes | Serving: 3

Ingredients

- ✓ ¼ cup of granulated sugar
- ✓ ½ tsp ground nutmeg
- ✓ 2 tsp ground cinnamon
- ✓ 1.5 cups of raw pecans
- ✓ ¼ cup of water
- ✓ 2 cups of raw almonds
- ✓ ½ tsp ground ginger
- ✓ ¾ cup of brown sugar

Instructions

1. Grease the bowl of the slow cooker a little. Put nuts in the crock pot.
2. Then, mix the sugars and cinnamon together in a small bowl and add them to the slow cooker. Mix everything well by stirring it together.
3. Then add water and stir again well.
4. For three hours, turn the slow cooker on HIGH. Turn it over every 20 to 30 minutes.
5. When they are done, put the nuts on a large sheet of parchment paper. Put nutmeg and ginger on top and gently toss. Let nuts cool all the way down. Keep it in a container that won't let air in.

23. QUICK CROCKPOT FONDUE

Prep Time: 5 Minutes | Cook Time: 20 Minutes

Total Time: 25 Minutes | Serving: 8

Ingredients

- ✓ 3 cloves garlic - peeled and crushed
- ✓ 1/2 tsp. nutmeg
- ✓ 1/8 tsp. cayenne pepper
- ✓ 1.5 pounds processed Swiss cheese - shredded or finely diced
- ✓ 3 cups of dry white wine - such as Chardonnay
- ✓ 1 tsp. ground white pepper

Instructions

1. Set a small slow cooker, like a Crockette, to "warm" and plug it in.
2. Boil the white wine and add the garlic cloves that have been crushed. Then add the cayenne pepper, ground white pepper, and nutmeg. Low-level the heat after five minutes and let it cook for ten minutes.
3. At the same time, put the processed Swiss cheese in the slow cooker and put the lid on top.
4. Pour the wine right over the cheese in the crock pot after 10 minutes of reducing it. Before you do this, you should take the crock off the heating element so that the liquid doesn't get on the electric parts.
5. Add the cheese to the wine mixture and mix it with a whisk. At first, it might look like it's not working, but it will soon. There should be no more big pieces after a few minutes. If there are, raise the heat to high and stir it around for 5 to 10 minutes until it is smooth.
6. Buns, rye or sourdough bread, or sausage should be served with it.

24. CHICKEN GNOCCHI SOUP

Prep Time: 10 Minutes | Cook Time: 8 Hour

Total Time: 8 Hour 10 Minutes | Serving: 10

Ingredients

- ✓ two 12 ounce cans evaporated milk
- ✓ 1 tsp salt
- ✓ 1–2 tsp dried basil
- ✓ 2 cups of fresh baby spinach
- ✓ 3 tbsp cornstarch dissolved in 2 tbsp water
- ✓ 1 pound boneless skinless chicken breasts
- ✓ 4 cups of chicken broth
- ✓ 2 cups of mirepoix (just a simple mixture of chopped onions, celery, and carrots)
- ✓ 1–2 tsp Italian seasoning
- ✓ 2–3 cloves garlic, minced
- ✓ two 1 pound packages gnocchi (about 4 cups)
- ✓ 1 tsp poultry seasoning
- ✓ 6 slices bacon

Instructions

1. Take a slow cooker or crockpot and add the chicken, mirepoix, basil, Italian seasoning, poultry seasoning, salt, and broth. Lock the lid on top and cook on high for four to five hours or low for six to eight hours. Take the chicken out of the pot and shred it in the casserole.
2. Together with the gnocchi, add the cornstarch mixture and the milk that has been evaporated. After stirring, put the cover back on. Once the soup has thickened and the gnocchi has softened, cook for another 45 minutes to an hour.
3. Break up the bacon into little pieces and fry them until they are crispy while the soup thickens. Remove the bacon from the pan and use paper towels to clean it. Save a little bacon for the spinach and garlic. It will take one minute after you add the garlic. Make sure to stir the spinach in until it's soft. Take it away from the fire. Cover the crock pot and add the bacon and spinach. Add everything together and mix well.
4. I added about a cup of water when it started to get thick and add more salt and pepper if you think it needs it.

25. TOMATO SOUP

Prep Time: 10 Minutes | Cook Time: 5 Hour 35 Minutes

Total Time: 5 Hour 45 Minutes | Serving: 6

Ingredients

- ✓ 1/3 cup of whole wheat orzo
- ✓ 1/2 tsp black pepper
- ✓ 1 can whole plum tomatoes (28 ounces) with juices
- ✓ 2 medium yellow onions chopped (about 3 cups)
- ✓ 3 cups of reduced-sodium chicken broth or vegetable broth
- ✓ 1 tsp hot Hungarian paprika
- ✓ 3 cloves garlic minced (about 1 tbsp)
- ✓ 2 tsp kosher salt
- ✓ 1 tbsp extra-virgin olive oil
- ✓ 1/4 cup of half-and-half optional

Instructions

1. Set the olive oil in a large pan over medium-low heat. Put the onions and cook for 15 minutes, mixing occasionally, until the onions are golden brown. For one more minute, add the garlic.
2. Spray some nonstick spray on a slow cooker that is at least 5 quarts in size. Include the onions and garlic that have been cooking. Put the chicken broth, tomatoes, salt, paprika, and black pepper on top, and then stir everything together. Put the lid on and cook on low for 5-6 hours or high for 2-3 hours until the tomatoes are perfectly soft. Make the soup smooth by using an immersion blender to blend it in. If you don't have an immersion blender, you can carefully move the soup to a food processor or blender and puree it in small amounts.
3. Turn up the heat to high and stir in the orzo. Cover and cook the orzo for about 20 to 30 minutes, stirring it twice or three times and checking to see if it's done. If you're using it, stir in the half-and-half. Add Parmesan and basil or parsley, if you like, and serve hot.

26. SEAFOOD STEW

Prep Time: 10 Minutes | Cook Time: 5 Hour

Total Time: 5 Hour 10 Minutes | Serving: 6

Ingredients

- ✓ 1 pound dutch baby potatoes
- ✓ 2 pounds seafood
- ✓ 1/2 tsp salt
- ✓ 1 tsp dried thyme
- ✓ 28 ounces crushed tomatoes
- ✓ 4 cups of vegetable broth
- ✓ 1/2 tsp pepper
- ✓ 1/2 tsp celery salt
- ✓ pinch cayenne pepper
- ✓ 1 tsp dried basil
- ✓ 1/4 tsp red pepper flakes
- ✓ 3 cloves minced garlic
- ✓ 1/2 medium onion diced
- ✓ 1 tsp dried cilantro
- ✓ 1/2 cup of white wine

Instructions

1. Put everything in the slow cooker except the seafood.
2. Put the lid on top and cook on high for two to three hours or low for four to six hours until the potatoes are soft.
3. Put seafood that has been thawed into the slow cooker and turn the heat back up to high. Cook the seafood for 30 to 60 minutes or until it's fully cooked.
4. As you like, serve with warm, crusty bread.

27. TACO SOUP

Prep Time: 20 Minutes | Cook Time: 4 Hour

Total Time: 4 Hour 20 Minutes | Serving: 8

Ingredients

- ✓ 1 (16 ounce) can pinto beans
- ✓ 1 pound (pound) ground beef
- ✓ 1 can tomatoes and chiles
- ✓ 1 (4 ounce) can diced green chiles
- ✓ 1 1/4 envelope envelope taco seasoning mix
- ✓ 1 (11 ounce) can niblet corn
- ✓ 1 envelope envelope Hidden Valley Ranch Salad Dressing and Seasoning Mix
- ✓ 1 (28 ounce) can diced tomatoes
- ✓ 1 can of white beans or kidney beans

Instructions

1. Make sure the meat is cooked by browning it first, then draining the liquid.
2. Put everything into your slow cooker. It has everything: beef, beans, corn, chilies, tomatoes, seasoning, and more. Keep in mind not to empty the cans! The flavors should be mixed together in the crock pot.
3. Put the food in the pot and cook on high for two hours or low for four to six hours. Add the toppings you like. Enjoy!

28. FRENCH ONION SOUP

Prep Time: 15 Minutes | Cook Time: 8 Hour

Total Time: 8 Hour 15 Minutes | Serving: 8

Ingredients

- ✓ 1 tsp Worcestershire sauce
- ✓ 1 tsp salt
- ✓ 8 slices of French bread
- ✓ 1 bay leaf
- ✓ 4 large yellow onions, sliced and separated into rings
- ✓ 4 shallots, sliced

- ✓ 8 cups of reduced-sodium beef broth
- ✓ 3 large cloves garlic, minced
- ✓ 1 tsp freshly cracked black pepper
- ✓ 1 tbsp fresh thyme
- ✓ ½ cup of sherry, or a dry red wine
- ✓ 8 thick slices Gruyere cheese, or Swiss
- ✓ 6 tbsp butter

Instructions

Caramelized Onions in Slow Cooker:

1. Put butter, onions, and shallots in a slow cooker and mix them together. For 8 to 10 hours, cook on low.

Caramelized Onions on Stovetop:

1. Melt the butter in a big pot with a heavy bottom over medium-high heat. After you add the onions and shallots, cook them for about 10 minutes until they become clear.
2. To make the onions brown and sweet, stir them around every few minutes for about 30 to 40 minutes. Put the caramelized onions in the slow cooker.

Crockpot French Onion Soup:

1. Spread out the onions that have been caramelized and add the garlic, sherry, beef stock, Worcestershire sauce, thyme, salt, pepper, and bay leaf.
2. Set the timer to high for 4-6 hours or low for 8-10 hours.
3. Set up a rack in the oven about 8 inches from the broiler and heat it up before you serve. Place bread slices on a baking sheet. Toast the bread slices in the broiler for about one to two minutes on each side. Take it out of the oven (but leave it on) and set it aside.
4. Put three-quarters of the way full of onion soup into oven-safe soup crocks and top each one with a toasted bread slice. Add a slice of cheese to the top of each bowl.
5. Put the bowls with food inside on a baking sheet. Cover with cheese topping. Broil for about 2 minutes or until it is lightly browned and bubbling. Serve right away.

29. CHICKEN PHO

Prep Time: 5 Minutes | Cook Time: 6 Hour 20 Minutes

Total Time: 6 Hour 25 Minutes | Serving: 6

Ingredients

- ✓ 2 inch piece fresh ginger peeled and thinly sliced
- ✓ 1-2 tsp kosher salt
- ✓ 8 cups of chicken stock
- ✓ bean sprouts
- ✓ 2 pounds boneless chicken breasts or bone-in would work too
- ✓ 8 star anise
- ✓ 3-4 cups of baby bok choy chopped
- ✓ fresh basil leaves
- ✓ 1 cinnamon stick
- ✓ lime wedges
- ✓ 2 tbsp fish sauce
- ✓ 6-8 ounce of pho rice noodles, banh pho 1/16 inch is the best, but whatever you can find will work!
- ✓ 1 1/2 tbsp light brown sugar
- ✓ hoisin
- ✓ 2 tsp whole coriander
- ✓ chili garlic sauce
- ✓ Sriracha
- ✓ 8 whole cloves
- ✓ sliced Jalapenos

Instructions

1. Insert the cinnamon stick, cloves, coriander, star anise, and cloves into a small pan that is heated over medium heat. Toast the nuts for about two minutes, stirring them often, until they smell good.
2. Crockpot chicken breasts that have been salted. Add ginger slices, fish sauce, and chicken stock. Mix the brown sugar in a little so it melts. Put in toasted spices.
3. On low for 6 to 8 hours or high for 3 to 4 hours, set the slow cooker to work.
4. Shuffle the chicken after taking it out of the crock pot. Take out the chicken and use a sieve to get rid of the ginger and whole spices.
5. Bring the chicken back to the crock pot and add the chopped bok choy. Open the lid and turn the heat up to high. Let it cook for another 15 minutes.
6. Slice the Jalapenos and lime wedges, and put the basil and sprouts on a plate while the bok choy cooks. Collect chili garlic sauce, hoisin, and sriracha.
7. After 15 minutes of cooking the bok choy, open the lid and add the dried rice noodles. Put the food in the broth and let it cook for 5 to 6 minutes or as long as the package says.
8. Pour pho into big bowls. Veggies, Jalapenos, or basil can be put on top. Depending on your preference, sprinkle sriracha, chili paste, or hoisin on top. Lastly, squeeze some fresh lime juice on top. Take it easy!!

30. VEGETARIAN LASAGNA SOUP

Prep Time: 20 Minutes | Cook Time: 3 Hour

Total Time: 3 Hour 20 Minutes | Serving: 8

Ingredients

- ✓ 4 cups of fresh spinach
- ✓ 6 ounces DeLallo lasagna noodles
- ✓ 2 zucchinis , sliced
- ✓ 3 tbsp DeLallo tomato paste
- ✓ 2 cups of brown mushrooms , sliced
- ✓ ⅛ tsp red pepper flakes
- ✓ 4 cups of vegetable broth
- ✓ 2 tsp dried oregano

- ✓ 2 tsp freshly ground black pepper
- ✓ 1 medium yellow onion , diced
- ✓ 1 tbsp extra virgin olive oil
- ✓ 2 tsp kosher salt
- ✓ 4 cloves garlic , minced or pressed
- ✓ 1 28 ounce can DeLallo crushed tomatoes
- ✓ 2 tsp dried basil
- ✓ 2 bay leaves

For the ricotta cheese topping:

- ✓ 8 ounces ricotta cheese
- ✓ ¼ cup of fresh basil leaves , chopped
- ✓ 1 cup of mozzarella cheese , shredded

- ✓ generous pinch of kosher salt
- ✓ ¼ cup of parsley , chopped

Instructions

For the lasagna soup:

1. Place the olive oil on medium heat in a skillet that doesn't stick. After adding the garlic, onion, and brown mushrooms, bake for four to five minutes or until the mushrooms get soft. Put the zucchini, crushed tomatoes, tomato sauce, vegetable broth, bay leaves, basil, oregano, red pepper flakes, kosher salt, and black pepper in the insert of a 6-quart slow cooker. Add the onion mixture.
2. If you set the slow cooker to low, it will cook for 7 hours. If you set it to high, it will cook for 3 ½ to 4 hours.
3. Just bake the lasagna noodles the way it says on the package when the time is up. Toss them in the soup after draining them. You can cut them up if you want to. Warm the spinach until it wilts. Put half of the ricotta cheese mixture and mix it in.
4. Add more parsley and basil on top of each bowl of soup after adding a dollop of the remaining ricotta cheese topping.

For the ricotta cheese topping:

1. Put everything in a small bowl and mix it all together. It should be kept in the fridge until it's time to serve.

31. CABBAGE ROLL SOUP

Prep Time: 20 Minutes | Cook Time: 3 Hour | Total Time: 3 Hour 20 Minutes | Serving: 12

Ingredients

- ✓ 28 ounces diced tomatoes
- ✓ 10 ounces tomato soup
- ✓ 5-6 cups of beef broth
- ✓ parsley for garnish
- ✓ 1 pound lean ground beef
- ✓ 1 pound thick bacon diced
- ✓ 1 tsp paprika
- ✓ 1 tbsp Worcestershire sauce
- ✓ 1 tsp thyme
- ✓ ⅔ cup of uncooked long grain rice
- ✓ salt and pepper to taste
- ✓ 6-8 cups of cabbage chopped
- ✓ 3 cloves garlic minced
- ✓ 1 large onion diced
- ✓ 1 ½ cups of V8/other vegetable juice
- ✓ 2 tbsp tomato paste

Instructions

1. In a pan, cook the bacon until it's nice and brown. Put it on paper towels to drain, and leave about a tbsp of bacon grease in the pan.
2. In the bacon fat, brown the beef and onion. Drain the extra fat after the meat is browned and put it in a 6qt (or bigger) slow cooker.
3. Put everything else into the slow cooker and mix it all together. The pot will be very full at this point.
4. Put the lid on top and cook on high for three to four hours or low for six to seven hours or until the rice is done. Add half of the cooked bacon and mix it in.
5. Put it in bowls and, if you want, top with the rest of the bacon and parsley.

32. MINESTRONE SOUP

Prep Time: 15 Minutes | Cook Time: 45 Minutes | Total Time: 1 Hour | Serving: 8

Ingredients

- ✓ 2 garlic cloves, minced
- ✓ 1 28 ounce can petite diced tomatoes
- ✓ 1/2 cup of diced celery
- ✓ 2 cups of cooked small pasta such as ditalini, al dente (or GF pasta)
- ✓ 2 cups of chopped fresh, or frozen defrosted spinach
- ✓ 1/2 tsp kosher salt and fresh black pepper
- ✓ 2 bay leaves
- ✓ 1 medium zucchini, 8 ounce each, diced
- ✓ Parmesan cheese rind, optional
- ✓ extra parmesan cheese for garnish, optional
- ✓ 1 15 ounce can white beans, drained, rinsed (cannellini or navy)
- ✓ 32 ounce container reduced sodium chicken broth, or vegetable broth for vegetarians
- ✓ 2 tsp olive oil
- ✓ 1/4 cup of chopped fresh Italian parsley
- ✓ 1/2 cup of chopped onion
- ✓ 2 tbsp chopped fresh basil
- ✓ 1 fresh rosemary sprig
- ✓ 1 cup of diced carrot

Instructions

Slow Cooker Version:

1. In a blender, blend the beans with 1 cup of the broth. Put the oil in a big nonstick skillet and heat it over medium-high heat. Put in the garlic, onion, carrots, and celery. Saute for about 15 minutes until the vegetables are soft and smell good.
2. Add the rest of the broth, tomatoes, pureed beans, parmesan cheese rind, salt, and pepper to the crock pot. Add the basil, parsley, rosemary, and bay leaves to cover the pot. Set the heat to low and let it cook for 6 to 8 hours.
3. Add the spinach and zucchini forty minutes before the soup is done cooking. Add the lid and cook for 30 more minutes. Get rid of the bay leaves, rosemary sprig, and parmesan rind. Add salt and black pepper to taste. Put 1-1/4 cups of soup and 1/4 cup of pasta into each of 8 bowls. You may include more Parmesan cheese if you choose.

Stove Top Directions:

1. In a blender, blend the beans with 1 cup of the broth. In a big pot, heat the oil over medium-high heat. Put in the garlic, onion, carrots, and celery. Saute for about 15 minutes until the vegetables are soft and smell good.
2. Put the rest of the broth, the tomatoes, the beans that have been pureed, the Parmesan cheese rind, salt, and pepper. Put in the basil, parsley, rosemary, bay leaves, and cover. Set the heat to low and cook for 40 minutes. Put in the spinach and zucchini. Cover and cook for 8-10 minutes or until the zucchini is soft.
3. Get rid of the rosemary sprig, bay leaves, and parmesan rind. Add salt and black pepper to taste. Put 1-1/4 cups of soup and 1/4 cup of pasta into each of 8 bowls. You can cover it with more Parmesan cheese.

Instant Pot Directions:

1. In a blender, blend the beans with 1 cup of the broth. In the Instant Pot, press "saute" and heat the oil. Put in the garlic, onion, carrots, and celery. Saute for about 10 minutes until the vegetables are soft and smell good.
2. Put the rest of the broth, the tomatoes, the beans that have been pureed, the Parmesan cheese rind, salt, and pepper. Cover and cook on high pressure for 20 minutes. Then add the basil, parsley, rosemary, bay leaves, and bay leaves.
3. After the quick release, put the pasta, zucchini, and spinach in the pot and cook on high for 4 minutes. Make a quick release so the pasta only cooks for a short time.
4. Get rid of the rosemary sprig, bay leaves, and parmesan rind. Add salt and black pepper to taste. Put 1-1/2 cups of soup into each of 8 bowls. If you want, add more Parmesan cheese on top.

33. PAULA DEEN'S POTATO SOUP

Prep Time: 10 Minutes | Cook Time: 6 Hour

Total Time: 6 Hour 10 Minutes | Serving: 6

Ingredients

- ✓ 1/3 tsp ground black pepper
- ✓ 1 bag frozen hash-brown potatoes
- ✓ 1/2 cup of onion (chopped)
- ✓ 1 (8 ounce) package cream cheese
- ✓ 2 (14 ounce) cans chicken broth
- ✓ 1 can cream of chicken soup
- ✓ Garnish: minced green onion, Cheddar, shredded, and bacon

Instructions

1. In a crockpot, mix the chicken broth, cream of chicken soup, chopped onions, grated black pepper, and frozen hash browns.
2. Lower the heat and cover the pot. Leave it to cook for 5 hours.
3. Include 8 ounces (1 package) of cream cheese that has been melted. Stir every now and then for another 30 minutes to make sure everything is mixed.
4. Add shredded Cheddar cheese, bacon strips, and minced green onion on top if you want to, but it's not required.

34. TORTELLINI SOUP

Prep Time: 5 Minutes | Cook Time: 3 Hour

Total Time: 3 Hour 5 Minutes | Serving: 6

Ingredients

- ✓ 1 (11-ounce) bag fresh spinach
- ✓ 6 cups of low-sodium chicken broth
- ✓ 2 (14.5-ounce) cans Italian-style diced tomatoes
- ✓ 1 tsp garlic salt
- ✓ 1 (8-ounce) package cream cheese cut into 1-inch cubes
- ✓ 1 (18-20-ounce) package three-cheese tortellini
- ✓ pepper to taste
- ✓ 1 tsp dried oregano
- ✓ 1 tsp ground cumin

Instructions

1. Put the tomatoes, spinach, cream cheese, cumin, oregano, garlic salt, and pepper into the slow cooker to taste.
2. On high for two to three hours, stirring every now and then, cover and cook.
3. After adding the tortellini, cook on high for another hour. Warm it up first.

35. VEGETARIAN CHILI

Prep Time: 15 Minutes | Cook Time: 4 Hour

Total Time: Minutes | Serving: 8

Ingredients

- ✓ 1 red bell pepper diced
- ✓ 1/2 tbsp salt plus more to taste
- ✓ 1/2 red onion diced
- ✓ 2 (4 ounce) cans diced green chiles
- ✓ 1 (15 ounce) can garbanzo beans rinsed and drained
- ✓ 1 (15 ounce) can black beans rinsed and drained
- ✓ 1 tsp ground black pepper
- ✓ 2 tsp garlic powder
- ✓ 1 sweet potato peeled and diced
- ✓ 1 cup of water
- ✓ 2 1/2 tbsp chili powder
- ✓ 1 (15 ounce) can kidney beans rinsed and drained
- ✓ 1 (8 ounce) can tomato sauce
- ✓ 1 (15 ounce) can diced tomatoes
- ✓ 1 green bell pepper diced
- ✓ 1 tbsp ground cumin
- ✓ 1 carrot diced
- ✓ 2 tsp dried oregano
- ✓ 2 stalks celery diced

Instructions

1. Spray cooking spray on the crock pot.
2. Add everything to the crockpot and stir until everything is mixed together.
3. Cover up. For 4 hours on HIGH or 8 hours on LOW, cook until the vegetables are soft. If you need to, taste and add more seasoning.
4. Top your chili with all of your favorite things.
5. Thanks for taking the time to rate this recipe. We appreciate it very much!

36. VEGETARIAN ENCHILADA CASSEROLE

Prep Time: 20 Minutes | Cook Time: 4 Hour

Total Time: 4 Hour | Serving: 6

Ingredients

- ✓ 1 zucchini, chopped
- ✓ 1 (12 ounce) can red enchilada sauce
- ✓ 1 bell pepper, chopped
- ✓ 1 (15 ounce) can diced fired roasted tomatoes
- ✓ 1/8 tsp
- ✓ 1 jalapeno, seeds removed and chopped
- ✓ 1 (15 ounce) can pinto beans, drained
- ✓ 1 cup of corn (fresh or frozen)
- ✓ 8 ounces shredded cheddar cheese
- ✓ 1/2 onion, chopped
- ✓ 1 tsp
- ✓ 9 (6" round) flour tortillas OR 3 large (10" burrito size tortillas)

Instructions

1. Mix the enchilada sauce and tomato dice in a small bowl, then set them aside.
2. Put the onion, zucchini, pepper, Jalapeno, and garlic, along with any other vegetables you want to use, into a large bowl. Also, put the corn and kidney beans in the bowl. Add salt and pepper, then toss to mix.
3. Fill the slow cooker with 1/4 cup of the enchilada sauce and tomato mix. Stack three flour tortillas on top of each other. (2 tortillas fit next to each other, and the third was cut in half to fill in the blanks.)
4. Put in half of the chopped vegetables and a quarter of the sauce and tomato mix. Add a third of the cheese, and then do it again.
5. Wraps, sauce, and cheese should be put on top one last time. Use a knife to make a few holes in the top tortilla to let some steam escape. The top layer will puff up as it cooks if you don't.
6. Put the lid on top and cook on low for 4 hours.
7. Set it to "keep warm" until you're ready to serve.
8. Add sour cream, chopped cilantro, and hot sauce to the dish before serving.

37. BAKED POTATOES

Prep Time: 5 Minutes | Cook Time: 4 Hour

Total Time: 4 Hour 5 Minutes | Serving: 4

Ingredients

- ✓ 2 tsp olive oil
- ✓ salt to taste
- ✓ 4 large russet or Idaho potatoes -3/4 pound / potato
- ✓ pepper to taste

Instructions

1. First, get the russet potatoes ready. Put potatoes in warm water and use your fingers to scrub off any leftover food or dirt.
2. Utilize a kitchen towel or a paper towel to dry. Penetrate all sides of the potatoes with a fork, about 8–10 times per potato.
3. Apply olive oil to each potato. Add as much salt and pepper as you like to the outside of each potato.
4. Put the potatoes in the slow cooker's bottom. Open the slow cooker's lid and set the temperature to high. For 4 to 6 hours, set the timer to maximum heat. The potatoes' size will affect how long they take to cook.
5. When you can poke a hole in a potato with a fork, and it comes out clean, the potatoes are done. To make them softer on the inside, cook them a little longer.
6. After baking the potatoes, let them cool for 10 to 15 minutes. Then, cut them up and serve.

38. CREAMY SPINACH TORTELLINI SOUP

Prep Time: 20 Minutes | Cook Time: 5 Hour

Total Time: 5 Hour 20 Minutes | Serving: 4

Ingredients

- ✓ 4 cups of low-sodium vegetable broth (32 ounces)
- ✓ 1 bay leaf
- ✓ 12 ounces cheese tortellini
- ✓ 28 ounces crushed tomatoes
- ✓ 1/2 tsp dried basil
- ✓ 1/4 cup of grated Parmesan cheese (1 ounce)
- ✓ 2 medium cloves garlic
- ✓ 2 medium carrots (peeled and chopped; about 3/4 cup)
- ✓ 1/2 tsp dried oregano
- ✓ 1/2 medium yellow onion
- ✓ 1/2 cup of shredded mozzarella cheese (2 ounces)
- ✓ 1/2 tsp black pepper
- ✓ 1 cup of half-and-half
- ✓ 4 ounces baby spinach
- ✓ 1 tsp kosher salt

Instructions

1. Place the slow cooker on low and add the tomatoes, onion, garlic, spices, and broth.
2. Cover and cook on low for 3 to 6 hours or longer if your slow cooker has a different time setting. It will be okay if you cook it for longer (like 8 hours).
3. Put the tortellini in the slow cooker, mix it in, cover it, and cook on high for 20 minutes.
4. Stir the spinach in until it wilts, then put the lid back on and cook for another 5 minutes.
5. Put the half-and-half in the microwave for 30 seconds to warm it up. You can put the cream, mozzarella, and Parmesan cheese in the slow cooker. Turn off the heat and stir until everything is well-mixed.
6. Take out the bay leaf. To taste, put more salt and pepper to the food.

39. SWEET POTATO BLACK BEAN PUMPKIN CHILI

Prep Time: 10 Minutes | Cook Time: 4 Hour

Total Time: 4 Hour | Serving: 6-8

Ingredients

- ✓ 1 cup of chopped onion (about 1 medium)
- ✓ 2 (14 ounce) canned black beans, drained and rinsed
- ✓ 1 (14 ounce) canned petite diced tomatoes (not drained)
- ✓ 1 (14 ounce) canned pumpkin
- ✓ 4 cups of sweet potato, peeled and chopped, about 1″ cubes (about 2 large potatoes)
- ✓ 1/2 tbsp minced garlic
- ✓ 3 cups of vegetable stock

Seasonings:

- ✓ 1 tsp cumin
- ✓ 1/2 tsp paprika
- ✓ 2 tbsp chili powder
- ✓ 1/4 tsp cayenne pepper
- ✓ 1 tsp salt (more or less, to taste)
- ✓ 1/8 tsp cinnamon

Toppings:

- ✓ vegan cheese or sour cream
- ✓ cilantro
- ✓ tortilla chips
- ✓ vegan cornbread
- ✓ avocado

Instructions

1. Put black beans, pumpkin, sweet potatoes, onion, minced garlic, small diced tomatoes, and vegetable stock in a crock pot. Add all of your seasonings and salt to taste. You can add more salt if you want. Stir the ingredients around until they are well mixed.
2. Set the timer to high for 4 hours or low for 6 to 8 hours. Top with and serve with your favorite sides and toppings.

40. VEGAN LENTIL TACOS

Prep Time: 10 Minutes | Cook Time: 8 Hour

Total Time: 8 Hour 10 Minutes | Serving: 8

Ingredients

- ✓ 1 tsp dried oregano
- ✓ 1 tbsp coconut aminos, or sub soy sauce
- ✓ 1 tsp salt
- ✓ 1 tbsp dried parsley, or 1/4 cup of fresh
- ✓ ½ cup of finely chopped onion
- ✓ 1 tsp paprika
- ✓ 1 ½ cups of green or brown dry lentils, picked over and rinsed
- ✓ 3 tsp ground cumin
- ✓ taco toppings
- ✓ 1 tbsp apple cider vinegar
- ✓ 1 tbsp olive or avocado oil
- ✓ 3 cups of low-sodium vegetable broth
- ✓ 1 ¼ cup of salsa
- ✓ 8 medium tortillas

Instructions

1. Put the ingredients in your slow cooker together. Cover and stir a few times.
2. Set the timer to HIGH for 3–4 hours or LOW for 7–8 hours. Since every slow cooker or crockpot cooks a little differently, the exact time will depend on the one you use. Cooking is done once the lentils are soft and most of the liquid is gone.
3. Spread the lentil taco filling out on tortillas, rice, greens, or however you like to eat it. Use a slotted spoon to do this. Add your favorite taco toppings, like extra red onion, cilantro, sliced avocado, or anything else you like.
4. Let leftovers cool down, then put them in a container that won't let air in and put it in the fridge for up to three days.

41. RISOTTO WITH ASPARAGUS

Prep Time: 15 Minutes | Cook Time: 4 Hour

Total Time: 4 Hour 15 Minutes | Serving: 6

Ingredients

- ✓ 2 tbsp chopped fresh dill or thyme
- ✓ 1 bunch fresh asparagus
- ✓ 1 ½ tsp kosher salt divided
- ✓ 4 cups of vegetable broth
- ✓ 2 tbsp toasted pine nuts
- ✓ ¼ cup of grated Gruyere cheese
- ✓ ½ cup of grated Parmesan cheese
- ✓ 1 ½ cups of arborio rice
- ✓ ¼ cup of dry white wine
- ✓ 2 tbsp extra virgin olive oil
- ✓ 2 cups of thinly sliced leeks white and light green parts
- ✓ ¼ tsp black pepper

Instructions

1. Set the oil over medium heat in a large pan. Salt and add the leeks. It will take about 10 minutes of cooking until the leeks are soft and smell good.
2. To lightly toast the rice, add it to the pan and cook for a few more minutes. Add the wine and cook until it's used up.
3. Tip: Wait to wash the rice. Some of the starches are washed away, but the starches are what make risotto creamy.
4. Put the rice and leeks in the slow cooker, and then add the broth. Put the lid on top and set the heat to low for 4 hours.
5. If you can, stir it once every two hours.
6. Cut the asparagus into 1-inch pieces at the three-hour mark and add them to the risotto.
7. Add the cheeses and serve when the risotto is done, which should be about 4 hours. Different slow cookers work in different ways, so check the rice to see if it's done before adding the cheese. Add pine nuts on top.

42. MUSHROOM STROGANOFF

Prep Time: 10 Minutes | Cook Time: 20 Minutes

Total Time: 30 Minutes | Serving: 3

Ingredients

- ✓ 18 ounce sliced mushrooms
- ✓ 1/2 cup of unsweetened creamer or canned coconut milk
- ✓ 2 1/2 tsp minced garlic
- ✓ optional 1/4 tsp dried thyme
- ✓ 1/2 cup of diced onion
- ✓ 2/3 cup of vegetable broth
- ✓ 2 tsp oil, or oil spray
- ✓ salt and optional pepper
- ✓ 2-4 tbsp flour of choice, including spelt, white, rice, sorghum, or almond
- ✓ optional protein of choice, such as lentils, tofu, or chickpeas

Instructions

1. If you want the gravy to be thicker, use more flour. If the stroganoff gets too thick, add more broth. When I eat it by itself, I add 1/2 tsp of salt. When I use it as a gravy over pasta or grain, I add 1 tsp. To make the recipe in a slow cooker, just put everything in and set it to high for 3 to 4 hours.

2. While the pan is on medium heat, add the oil or spray and cook the onions until they start to turn brown. If you want, add garlic, salt, mushrooms, and thyme. Stir every so often. The mushrooms will become wet. Let it cook for about 10 minutes or until the pan starts to look dry again. Add the milk, flour, and broth and mix them together. Cook it, stirring it sometimes, until it gets thicker. I like to serve my coffee with extra milk or creamer.

43. VEGAN CHILI CHEESE LENTIL DIP

Prep Time: 15 Minutes | Cook Time: 5 Hour

Total Time: 5 Hour 15 Minutes | Serving: 8

Ingredients

- ✓ 1/2 orange bell pepper
- ✓ 1/4 cup of nutritional yeast
- ✓ 1/4 cup of canned diced green chilis, drained and rinsed
- ✓ extra salt to taste
- ✓ 1 3/4 tsp chili powder, divided
- ✓ 1 1/2 cups of vegetable stock
- ✓ 3/4 tsp cumin, divided
- ✓ 3/4 cup of diced tomatoes (about 1/2 14-ounce can)
- ✓ Tortilla chips for dipping
- ✓ optional: cilantro for garnish
- ✓ 1/4 tsp garlic powder
- ✓ 1/4 cup of diced onion
- ✓ 1 cup of cashews, soaked for at least two hours
- ✓ 1/2 tsp chipotle powder, divided
- ✓ 1/2 tsp salt, divided
- ✓ 1/2 cup of dry brown or green lentils
- ✓ 3/4 cup of hot almond milk

Instructions

1. Fill a slow cooker with vegetable stock, onion, tomatoes, lentils, chilis, garlic powder, 1/4 tsp cumin, 1/4 tsp chipotle powder, and 1 tsp chili powder. Put it in the oven on high for three to four hours or until most of the liquid is gone.
2. Put cashews, nutritional yeast, 3/4 tsp chili powder, 1/2 tsp cumin, 1/4 tsp chipotle powder, 1/4 tsp salt, and bell pepper in a food processor. Pulse for 3 to 5 minutes or until the mixture is smooth and creamy. As needed, add more salt.
3. Combine the cashew cheese with the lentils in the slow cooker. Warm dip should be served with tortilla chips, and cilantro can be added on top if you want to.

44. VEGGIE OMELET

Prep Time: 5 Minutes | Cook Time: 1 Hour 30 Minutes

Total Time: 1 Hour 35 Minutes | Serving: 4

Ingredients

- ✓ 1 tsp dried parsley
- ✓ Salt and pepper to taste
- ✓ 4 egg whites
- ✓ 1 cup of spinach shredded
- ✓ 1 cup of bell pepper diced (or 1 whole bell pepper diced)
- ✓ 1/2 cup of unsweetened almond milk
- ✓ 1 tsp garlic powder
- ✓ 1/2 cup of white onion diced
- ✓ 6 eggs

Instructions

1. Oil the inside of a slow cooker with cooking spray, or line it with plastic wrap to make it easy to take out and clean.
2. Whisk the milk, garlic powder, parsley, salt, and pepper into the eggs, egg whites, and eggs in a bowl. Include the bell peppers, onion, and spinach. This can be made with any vegetables. Cooked bacon or sausage would also be perfect.
3. Add the ingredients to the slow cooker.
4. 90 minutes on high. Check the eggs at 60 minutes to see if they are set. This is the length of time mine took. Wait 20 to 30 minutes more if it's not set. It's best to check because the timing will be different from one slow cooker to the next.
5. Cut it into four wedges and serve right away!

45. SKINNY VEGGIE LASAGNA

Prep Time: 15 Minutes | Cook Time: 6 Hour 15 Minutes

Total Time: 6 Hour 30 Minutes | Serving: 9

Ingredients

- ✓ 9 thick lasagna noodles with wavy edges (mine were called bronze cut)
- ✓ 3–4 cups of chopped vegetables of choice
- ✓ 2 cups of shredded Mozzarella or Provolone cheese
- ✓ 24 ounces part-skim ricotta cheese OR cottage cheese
- ✓ Parmesan cheese for topping
- ✓ Pesto (to taste)
- ✓ fresh parsley for topping
- ✓ 2 24-ounce jars or cans of Italian tomato sauce

Instructions

1. Use nonstick cooking spray on the crockpot. Put 1/2 cup of tomato sauce in the middle to keep the noodles from sticking.
2. Break up the noodles so that they fit and cover most of the bottom. It's not a big deal that they will look weird. Put about a third of the ricotta on top, then the vegetables, pesto, sauce, cheese, and finally the noodles. Do layers again and again until you have three full layers. Last, put a layer of noodles on top. Put a thin layer of sauce and a little more shredded cheese on top of that.
3. Put the lid on top and cook on high for three hours or low for five to six hours. Turn off the crockpot for at least an hour and let the lasagna sit there. This lets the lasagna soak up all the water. If you don't do this, it will turn out more like lasagna soup, which is still tasty but not very appealing. If you let it sit for a while, you can either use a spoon to take out pieces or cut it like the real thing.

46. LOBSTER BISQUE

Prep Time: 45 Minutes | Cook Time: 6 Hour 45 Minutes

Total Time: 7 Hour 30 Minutes | Serving: 6

Ingredients

- ✓ 1 Tsp Freshly Cracked Black Pepper
- ✓ 2 Shallots Finely Minced
- ✓ 1 Clove Garlic Finely Minced
- ✓ 1/4 Cup of Fresh Parsley Chopped
- ✓ 1 32 Ounce Carton Chicken Broth
- ✓ 2 14.5 Ounce Cans Petite Diced Tomatoes, With Juice

- ✓ 1 Pint Heavy Cream
- ✓ 4 Lobster Tails
- ✓ 1 Tsp Dried Dill
- ✓ 1 tbsp Old Bay Seasoning
- ✓ 1/2 Tsp Paprika!

Instructions

1. Minced shallots and garlic should be cooked in a small skillet until the shallots start to wilt and turn clear.
2. Put the garlic and shallot mixture into a crock pot that is at least 4 quarts in size. Then add the tomatoes, chicken broth, old bay seasoning, dill, parsley, pepper, and paprika.
3. Cut off the fan-shaped end of the lobsters with a very sharp knife and put them in the crock pot. Wait to eat the meaty part of the tail.
4. Put the lid on and cook on low for 6 hours or high for 3 hours.
5. Take the lobster tail ends out of the crock pot and throw them away.
6. Apply a blender or an immersion blender to blend the soup until it has the texture you want. Depending on your blender's size, you might have to do this in parts.
7. If you used a regular blender, put the soup back in the crock pot and add it now. The lobster meat should be added to the soup. Cover and cook on low for 45 minutes or until the shells turn red and the meat is done.
8. Take the lobster tails out of the soup and let them cool down a bit. Put the cream into the soup and stir it while the lobster cools.
9. Cut each lobster tail in half lengthwise with a sharp knife, then remove the meat from the shells.
10. Throw away the shells and chop the lobster meat into small pieces. Then, add the meat back to the soup. Serve and enjoy!

47. SHRIMP SCAMPI

Prep Time: 10 Minutes | Cook Time: 3 Hour

Total Time: 3 Hour 10 Minutes | Serving: 6

Ingredients

- ✓ 2 tbsp fresh parsley
- ✓ 1 cup of chicken broth or you can use water
- ✓ 2 pound shrimp frozen, precooked, deveined and peeled
- ✓ ½ cup of freshly grated parmesan cheese
- ✓ 1 tbsp garlic salt
- ✓ 16 ounce angel hair pasta
- ✓ 2 lemons freshly squeezed
- ✓ salt and pepper to taste

Instructions

1. In the crock pot, mix everything together except the parmesan cheese and the angel hair parsley.
2. Set the timer to low and leave it on for three to four hours.
3. Mix half of the Parmesan cheese in.
4. Put it on top of cooked angel hair pasta and sprinkle the rest of the parmesan cheese on top.

48. SPINACH AND CRAB LASAGNA

Prep Time: 15 Minutes | Cook Time: 2 Hour 45 Minutes

Total Time: 3 Hour | Serving: 8

Ingredients

- ✓ 1 (8 ounce) package imitation crabmeat
- ✓ 1 (16 ounce) package dried lasagna noodles
- ✓ 12 ounces ricotta cheese
- ✓ 15 fresh mushrooms, sliced
- ✓ 1 ½ cups of shredded mozzarella cheese
- ✓ 1 (16 ounce) jar Alfredo sauce
- ✓ 1 bunch fresh spinach, chopped
- ✓ 1 (12 ounce) container cottage cheese

Instructions

1. Pour half of the Alfredo sauce jar into the slow cooker. Add lasagna noodles on top of the sauce. Place a layer of spinach, then a layer of mushrooms, and finally, a layer of crabmeat on top of the lasagna noodles. Place half of the cottage cheese and half of the ricotta cheese on top of the crab meat. Add the rest of the ingredients one layer at a time, ending with noodles and Alfredo sauce on top.
2. Set the timer to 2 hours and 15 minutes on High. Put mozzarella cheese on top of the lasagna and cook on High for another 30 minutes or until the cheese melts.

49. TUNA CASSEROLE

Prep Time: 15 Minutes | Cook Time: 2 Hour

Total Time: 2 Hour 15 Minutes | Serving: 10

Ingredients

- ✓ 1 ½ tsp dried thyme
- ✓ 2 tbsp dried parsley flakes
- ✓ 1 cup of milk
- ✓ 10 ounce frozen peas thawed
- ✓ 4 ounce of pimentos diced
- ✓ salt and pepper to taste
- ✓ 2 cups of shredded cheddar cheese
- ✓ 14 ounce canned tuna two small cans
- ✓ ¼ cup of breadcrumbs
- ✓ 14 ounce egg noodles
- ✓ 2 cans cream of celery soup

Instructions

1. It's not quite a dente, but it's still chewy.
2. Toss everything in a very large bowl except for the breadcrumbs and 1 cup of shredded cheese. Put salt and pepper to taste to adjust the seasonings.
3. Then, grease the inside of a big slow cooker and put the mixed ingredients in it. Add the last bit of shredded cheese and breadcrumbs on top.
4. Place it in the oven on high for two hours or low for four to six hours with the lid on.

50. DILL HALIBUT

Prep Time: 5 Minutes | Cook Time: 1 Hour 30 Minutes

Total Time: 1 Hour 35 Minutes | Serving: 2

Ingredients

- ✓ 1 Tbsp olive oil
- ✓ 1 1/2 tsp dried dill or 1 Tbsp fresh dill
- ✓ Salt and pepper
- ✓ 12 ounce wild Alaska seafood halibut (fresh or frozen)
- ✓ 1 Tbsp fresh lemon juice

Instructions

1. Halibut should be put in the middle of a large 18-inch piece of nonstick foil. Spray nonstick cooking spray on your foil if it doesn't already have it. Add a little salt and pepper to the halibut.
2. Mix the olive oil, lemon juice, and dill in a small bowl with a whisk. Pour the sauce over the halibut.
3. Raise the foil's edges and crimp them together, but make sure there is a lot of space inside for the fish to steam. Then, I put the foil in the bottom of an oval 6-quart slow cooker and cooked on high for 90 minutes to two hours (my fish was frozen, so it took exactly two hours).
4. Watch out for steam when you open the foil package and check the fish to see if it's ready to eat. It'll be soft and flaky. Serve and have fun. I always put fresh lemon juice on top of my fish with you. A little sauteed spinach went with my fish, and I put fresh dill and diced tomatoes on top of the fish.

51. FISH CHOWDER

Prep Time: 15 Minutes | Cook Time: 6 Hour

Total Time: 6 Hour | Serving: 6

Ingredients

- ✓ 1/4 tsp freshly ground black pepper
- ✓ 1 medium onion, coarsely chopped
- ✓ 2 pounds frozen fish fillets, such as catfish, or haddock, thawed
- ✓ 2 cups of water
- ✓ 4 medium red-skinned potatoes, peeled and cubed
- ✓ 1 to 1 1/2 tsp kosher salt, or to taste
- ✓ 1/4 pound bacon, or streaky salt pork, diced
- ✓ 1 (12-ounce) can evaporated milk

Instructions

1. Get the ingredients together.
2. Cut the fish fillets into small pieces when they are no longer frozen.
3. Put it in the crock pot. Cut the salt pork or bacon into little chunks.
4. Place the chopped onion, bacon, or salt pork in a big skillet over medium-low heat. Fry the meat until it's done, and the onion turns golden.
5. Remove and throw away any extra fat.
6. Put the fish pieces, bacon, and onion mixture in the slow cooker.
7. Put in the water, salt, pepper, and cubed potatoes.
8. Turn the heat down to low, cover, and cook for 5 to 6 hours or until the potatoes are soft.
9. After you add the evaporated milk can, cook it for another 30 minutes to an hour or until it's hot. Serve and have fun.

52. SAUSAGE AND SHRIMP GUMBO

Prep Time: 20 Minutes | Cook Time: 6 Hour

Total Time: 6 Hour 20 Minutes | Serving: 6

Ingredients

- ✓ 1 (15 ounce) can diced tomatoes
- ✓ 2 stalks celery, diced
- ✓ 1/2 cup of diced onion
- ✓ 2-3 cloves garlic, minced
- ✓ 1/2 tsp dried thyme
- ✓ 1-2 tsp Cajun seasoning
- ✓ 14 ounces andouille sausage, sliced
- ✓ 2 bay leaves
- ✓ Hot cooked rice, for serving
- ✓ 1/4 cup of water
- ✓ 1 tbsp Worcestershire sauce
- ✓ 1 tsp hot sauce
- ✓ Salt and pepper, to taste
- ✓ 4 cups of chicken broth
- ✓ 1/2 tsp dried basil
- ✓ 1 bell pepper, diced
- ✓ 10 ounces shrimp, peeled and deveined
- ✓ 1 tbsp olive oil
- ✓ 1/4 cup of cornstarch
- ✓ 1/2 tsp dried oregano

Instructions

1. Put oil in a big pan and set it over medium heat. Put in the sausage, pepper, onion, celery, garlic, and saute until the sausage turns brown and the vegetables are soft. Put it in a slow cooker that has been lightly greased.
2. Place the chicken broth, spices, hot sauce, and Worcestershire sauce in a slow cooker. Add the diced tomatoes and stir to mix. Put the lid on top and set the heat to low.
3. Mix the cornstarch and water in a small bowl with a whisk about 30 minutes before you serve. Whisk the cornstarch mixture in a slow cooker until it is smooth. Put in shrimp. Put the lid back on and cook for another 20 to 30 minutes until the shrimp is done and the gumbo has thickened a bit. Put it on top of hot rice.

53. SHRIMP FAJITAS

Prep Time: 5 Minutes | Cook Time: 5 Hour

Total Time: 5 Hour 5 Minutes | Serving: 4

Ingredients

- ✓ 2 red peppers sliced
- ✓ 1 onion sliced
- ✓ 1/2 tsp paprika
- ✓ 1 taco seasoning packet
- ✓ 1 pound raw shrimp deveined and peeled
- ✓ 1 to mato quartered
- ✓ 1/2 cup of chicken broth
- ✓ 1 tsp salt
- ✓ 2 green peppers sliced
- ✓ 1 tsp chili powder

Instructions

1. Add everything except the shrimp to the crockpot and cook on low for 5 to 6 hours.
2. Put the shrimp in the slow cooker next. Mix them well, then turn it on high for another 30 to 45 minutes. Put it on tortillas and top with your favorite things.

54. CRAB ARTICHOKE DIP

Prep Time: 10 Minutes | Cook Time: 2 Hour 30 Minutes

Total Time: 2 Hour 40 Minutes | Serving: 12

Ingredients

- ✓ 1 tbsp lemon juice
- ✓ 1/2 tsp garlic powder
- ✓ 1 (12-ounce) jar marinated artichoke hearts, drained and chopped
- ✓ 2 tsp Worcestershire sauce
- ✓ 1/2 tsp crushed red pepper flakes
- ✓ 1 cup of shredded Parmesan cheese
- ✓ 1/2 tsp Old Bay seasoning
- ✓ 2 green onions, sliced
- ✓ 1/2 cup of shredded mozzarella cheese
- ✓ 12 ounces fresh or canned crab meat, drained
- ✓ 1/3 cup of chopped roasted red peppers
- ✓ 12 ounces cream cheese, softened
- ✓ 1/2 cup of mayonnaise

Instructions

1. Mix everything in a 3 to 4-quart slow cooker EXCEPT the green onions.
2. Set the temperature to low and cover the pan. Halfway through, I like to stir it. After serving, sprinkle green onions on top.

55. SALMON FILLETS & ASIAN VEGETABLES

Prep Time: 10 Minutes | Cook Time: 3 Hour

Total Time: 3 Hour 10 Minutes | Serving: 2

Ingredients

- ✓ 1 package (12 to 16 ounces) frozen Asian stir fry vegetable blend
- ✓ 2 tbsp lemon juice
- ✓ 2 tbsp honey
- ✓ 10 ounces salmon fillets
- ✓ 1 tsp sesame seeds (optional)
- ✓ 2 tbsp soy sauce (gluten-free, if desired)
- ✓ Salt & Pepper

Instructions

1. A 1-½-quart slow cooker is the best size.
2. Put the vegetables that have been frozen in the slow cooker.
3. Put salt and pepper to taste to the salmon.
4. Food should be put on top of the salmon.
5. Mix the honey, soy sauce, and lemon juice together, then pour it over the salmon. If you want, sprinkle with sesame seeds.
6. Put the lid on top and set the temperature to LOW for two to three hours or until the salmon is done the way you like it. I really enjoy salmon, so I like it just barely done. Mine took about 2 and a half hours to cook. If you want, serve with brown rice.
7. Put the sauce from the slow cooker to everything.

56. EASY JAMBALAYA

Prep Time: 10 Minutes | Cook Time: 4 Hour | Total Time: 4 Hour 10 Minutes | Serving: 8

Ingredients

- ✓ ½ tsp dried thyme
- ✓ 1 cup of celery chopped
- ✓ 1 (28-ounce) can diced tomatoes
- ✓ 1 medium green bell pepper chopped
- ✓ salt and pepper to taste
- ✓ 1 tbsp parsley
- ✓ 1 pound raw peeled and deveined medium shrimp thawed if frozen
- ✓ 1 (12-ounce) package smoked sausage , sliced
- ✓ 1 small onion chopped
- ✓ 1 tbsp Creole seasoning
- ✓ optional: red pepper sauce for more heat!

Instructions

1. Spray nonstick spray on the slow cooker. Dice the tomatoes, add smoked sausage, creole seasoning, parsley, and thyme. Also, add the onion, bell pepper, and celery. Move it around a little.
2. Cover and cook on the low setting for three to four hours or until the vegetables are soft.
3. Put the thawed shrimp into the slow cooker and cook for another 30 minutes or until the shrimp are pink. Depending on your taste, put salt and pepper. Add some red pepper hot sauce if you want it to be spicier. Happy eating!

57. PORK ROAST WITH GRAVY

Prep Time: 5 Minutes | Cook Time: 5 Hour | Total Time: 5 Hour 5 Minutes | Serving: 6

Ingredients

- ✓ 10.5 ounce cream of mushroom soup
- ✓ 1 yellow onion, sliced
- ✓ 10.5 ounce cream of chicken soup
- ✓ 2 cups of carrots
- ✓ 3 pound Pork Shoulder
- ✓ .87 ounce packet pork gravy mix
- ✓ Pork Seasoning:
- ✓ 3/4 tsp oregano
- ✓ 3/4 tsp thyme
- ✓ 1 tsp rosemary
- ✓ 1/8 tsp nutmeg
- ✓ 1/8 tsp pepper
- ✓ 3/4 tsp sage

Instructions

1. In the slow cooker, mix the soup mix and gravy mix together.
2. Use paper towels to dry the pork, and then press the seasoning mix firmly onto the pork's surface.
3. Put the pork, carrots, and onions that have been sliced into the slow cooker. Set the timer to 5 hours on high or 8 hours on low. Enjoy with potatoes!

58. CHEESY HAMBURGER HASH

Prep Time: 15 Minutes | Cook Time: 8 Hour

Total Time: 8 Hour 15 Minutes | Serving: 4

Ingredients

- ✓ 2 cups of potatoes pared and diced
- ✓ 3/4 cups of shredded sharp cheddar cheese
- ✓ 1/4 cup of diced green bell pepper
- ✓ 1/2 cup of beef broth/stock
- ✓ 1/4 cup of diced red bell pepper
- ✓ 1 1/2 pounds lean ground beef
- ✓ 1 - 8 ounce can tomato sauce
- ✓ 1/4 cup of chopped onion
- ✓ 10.75 ounce can cream of mushroom soup

Instructions

1. Prepare ground beef by browning it and then removing any extra fat.
2. Cook the ground beef and add the potatoes, tomato sauce, soup, peppers, onion, and beef stock. Mix everything together in a large bowl.
3. For a 4-6 quart slow cooker, put it in.
4. Lower the heat and let it cook for 6 to 8 hours.
5. Put in the cheese and stir it in until it melts. Serve right away.

59. PULLED PORK TACOS

Prep Time: 10 Minutes | Cook Time: 4 Hour

Total Time: 4 Hour 10 Minutes | Serving: 6

Ingredients

- ✓ 1 4-pound boneless pork shoulder roast
- ✓ 1 tbsp ground cumin
- ✓ salt to taste
- ✓ 1 small onion - peeled and cut in half
- ✓ 1 tbsp smoked paprika
- ✓ 1 cup of prepared salsa - (use your favorite!)
- ✓ 1 canned chipotle chili + 2 tbsp of the adobo sauce from the can
- ✓ 10-12 6-inch tortillas
- ✓ 3 tsp minced garlic
- ✓ favorite toppings such as lettuce, cheese, hot sauce, green onions, cilantro, or lime wedges - optional, for serving

Instructions

1. Cut the pork into 4 pieces and remove any extra fat. Sprinkle a lot of salt on all sides.
2. Add the chipotle chili, adobo sauce, cumin, smoked paprika, garlic, and 1 tsp of salt to a slow cooker. Stir the ingredients together.
3. Put the pork and onion in the slow cooker. Cover and turn the meat to coat it with the sauce. Set the timer for 4 hours on high or 6 hours on low.
4. Put the pork in a bowl and use two forks to shred it. You can skim the fat off the top of the sauce with a spoon or a fat separator. Put on enough sauce to keep the pork moist.
5. Heat the tortillas up to serve, and add the pulled pork and any toppings you like.

60. STUFFED CABBAGE ROLLS

Prep Time: 25 Minutes | Cook Time: 8 Hour 20 Minutes

Total Time: 8 Hour 45 Minutes | Serving: 6

Ingredients

- ✓ 1 cup of cooked rice
- ✓ 2 tbsp brown sugar, packed
- ✓ 1 tsp fine salt
- ✓ 1 1/2 tsp Worcestershire sauce
- ✓ 1/4 tsp freshly ground black pepper
- ✓ 1 (15-ounce) can tomato sauce
- ✓ 2 slices bacon, chopped
- ✓ 2 tbsp lemon juice, from 1/2 large lemon
- ✓ 1 pound lean ground beef
- ✓ 1/4 cup of milk
- ✓ 1 pound ground pork
- ✓ 1 large egg, beaten
- ✓ 1/4 cup of chopped onion, from 1/2 medium onion
- ✓ 1 head green cabbage, 1 to 2 pounds

Instructions

1. Get the things you need.
2. In a dish that can go in the microwave, put the cabbage head. For about 14 minutes, cook the cabbage on high in the microwave. Peel the cabbage leaves off when they're cool enough to touch.
3. Fry the bacon in a small skillet over medium-low heat until it's crispy. Take the bacon out of the pan and put it somewhere else. You don't need to drain the bacon because you will use it along with the fat in step 6.
4. Put the beef, pork, milk, onion, rice, salt, pepper, and beaten egg in a big bowl. Be sure to mix the ingredients well.
5. Put a cabbage leaf with 1/4 cup of the meat mixture on it. You can use toothpicks to hold it together if you want to, and then roll it up like a burrito and put it in the crock pot seam side down. Do the same thing with the rest of the leaves and meat mixture.
6. Combine the Worcestershire sauce, brown sugar, lemon juice, and tomato sauce in a small bowl.
7. The sauce should be poured over the cabbage rolls. Add the bacon and the fat. It should be cooked on low for 7-9 hours or high for 4-5 hours or until the meat is done. A digital thermometer should read 160 F for the filling.
8. Carefully place the cabbage rolls on a platter or individual plates, and then pour the tomato sauce on top of them.

61. PORK CARNITAS BURRITO BOWLS

Prep Time: 10 Minutes | Cook Time: 3 Hour

Total Time: 3 Hour 10 Minutes | Serving: 12

Ingredients

Pork Carnitas:

- ✓ 2 tsp dried oregano
- ✓ 4 medium garlic cloves, minced
- ✓ 1 tsp ground cumin
- ✓ 3 medium limes, juiced
- ✓ 2 tsp kosher salt
- ✓ 1 cup of chicken or vegetable stock
- ✓ 3-4 pounds boneless pork shoulder
- ✓ 2 small tomatoes
- ✓ ½ cups of orange juice, or juice from 2 oranges
- ✓ 1 tbsp chili powder

Pineapple-Cucumber Salsa:

- ✓ ½ medium red onion, finely chopped
- ✓ ¼ cup of chopped fresh cilantro leaves
- ✓ ½ pineapple, peeled and chopped
- ✓ ½ medium long English cucumber
- ✓ 1 medium Jalapeno, chopped, optional
- ✓ 1 pinch fine sea salt

Burrito Bowls:

- ✓ 4 cups of cooked rice

Optional garnishes:

- ✓ ½ medium avocado, sliced
- ✓ 2 tbsp chopped cilantro
- ✓ ½ cup of sour cream
- ✓ 1 cup of guacamole
- ✓ 1 cup of chopped tomatoes or chunky salsa

Instructions

Slow Cooker Pork Carnitas:

1. Put kosher salt, chili powder, oregano, and cumin in a small bowl and mix them together. After rubbing the pork shoulder all over, put it in the slow cooker. Put orange juice, lime juice, garlic, tomatoes, stock, and orange juice into the slow cooker.
2. The food will be ready after 3-4 hours on high or 6-8 hours on low.
3. It's time to shred the pork. You can use two forks or your hands to do this. Take out any big pieces of fat and throw them away.
4. Put the meat and its juices in the slow cooker and mix everything together.
5. Heat up the oven's broiler. Put the meat on a foil-covered baking sheet. Some of the juices will stay in the slow cooker and can be thrown away. Put the meat under the broiler for 5 to 10 minutes or until the pork crisps and the top browns even more.

Instant Pot Pork Carnitas:

1. About 4 to 6 smaller pieces of pork should be cut up.
2. Put kosher salt, chili powder, oregano, and cumin in a small bowl and mix them together. Apply the rub all over the pork shoulder.
3. Put in orange juice, lime juice, garlic, tomatoes, stock, and orange juice.
4. Season the pork and put it in the instant pot. You don't need a trivet.
5. Seal the valve and close the Instant Pot. Cook on HIGH PRESSURE for 22 minutes. Let it happen naturally.
6. Open the Instant Pot's lid carefully once the valve has dropped naturally and the lid is no longer locked. It's time to shred the pork. You can use two forks or your hands to do this. Take out any big pieces of fat and throw them away.
7. Put the meat and juices back into the Instant Pot and mix everything.
8. Warm up the oven's broiler. Some of the meat's juices will stay in the Instant Pot. Put the meat on a baking sheet lined with foil and broil under the broiler for 5 to 10 minutes, or until the pork starts to crisp and the top starts to brown even more.

Pineapple-Cucumber Salsa:

1. Mix the jalapeno, pineapple, cucumber, red onion, cilantro, and red onion in a bowl. Sprinkle with a little bit of salt and toss to mix.

Burrito Bowls:

2. Mix the rice, salsa, and pork carnitas in a bowl. Add any toppings you want on top.

62. TACO MEAT

Prep Time: 5 Minutes | Cook Time: 5 Hour

Total Time: 5 Hour 5 Minutes | Serving: 2

Ingredients
- ✓ 2 pounds ground beef
- ✓ 1.5cups of diced tomatoes with juice
- ✓ 1.5tsp garlic powder
- ✓ 1/2 tsp black pepper
- ✓ 1 tsp chili powder
- ✓ 1 cup of mild green chilis, diced
- ✓ 1.5tsp sea salt
- ✓ 1 tsp ground cumin
- ✓ 1 tsp smoked paprika
- ✓ 1 small onion, diced

Instructions

1. Put everything in a slow cooker.
2. Warm the food on HIGH for two to four hours or until it turns golden brown. It should be stirred and broken up every once in a while. Before you eat, set the crock pot to LOW or WARM if the food is done cooking before you are.
3. You can cook the taco meat on LOW for 6 to 8 hours if you want to get ahead of time.

63. PORK & SAGE RAGU

Prep Time: 20 Minutes | Cook Time: 5 Hour

Total Time: 5 Hour 20 Minutes | Serving: 6

Ingredients

- 250g carrots peeled and diced
- 300g pork shoulder steaks (approx 2 steaks)
- 500g pork mince (lean)
- 1 tbsp tomato puree
- 250 ml chicken or vegetable stock
- 1 tsp dried sage
- 1 tsp mustard powder
- 1 tsp sea salt
- 2 tsp Worcestershire sauce
- 1 onion diced
- 400g tinned tomatoes (1 tin)
- ¼ tsp black pepper
- 3 cloves garlic
- 2 tsp fresh sage
- 2 sticks celery

Instructions

1. On the stove (if your slow cooker has a hob), in a pan, or in the slow cooker pan itself, brown the pork mince. It could take 5 minutes.
2. Place the pork shoulder steaks on top of the mince that has been browned.
3. The onion, carrots, and celery should all be peeled and cut into small pieces. Put it in the slow cooker with the rest of the ingredients.
4. Give it a good stir, and set it to high for 5 to 6 hours.
5. Before putting the pork shoulder back in the slow cooker, take it out and shred it. Really mix it up.

64. MISSISSIPPI PORK ROAST

Prep Time: 5 Minutes | Cook Time: 6 Hour

Total Time: 6 Hour 5 Minutes | Serving: 6

Ingredients

- 1 packet au jus gravy mix
- 2 pounds marinated fresh pork roast
- 1 packet ranch seasonings
- 1/2 stick butter
- 8-10 pepperoncini peppers

Instructions

1. Put the pork roast in the cooking pot. Place ranch and au jus packs on top. Put butter and pepper on top. Set the heat to low and leave it alone for six hours. Use a fork to shred it, then serve.

65. HONEY GARLIC MEATBALLS

Prep Time: 10 Minutes | Cook Time: 3 Hour | Total Time: 3 Hour 10 Minutes | Serving: 6

Ingredients

- ✓ 1/2 tsp black pepper
- ✓ 1 tsp salt
- ✓ 1/2 cup of plain breadcrumbs
- ✓ 1/2 cup of onion

- ✓ 3 cloves garlic, minced
- ✓ 1 whole large egg
- ✓ 1 pound ground beef

Honey Garlic Sauce:

- ✓ 1/2 cup of ketchup
- ✓ 1/3 cup of honey
- ✓ 1/2 cup of soy sauce

- ✓ 1 Tbsp fresh chopped cilantro
- ✓ 1/2 Tbsp sesame seeds
- ✓ 4 cloves garlic, minced

Instructions

1. Set the oven to broil.
2. Mix everything that goes into the meatballs together. Make meatballs about the size of golf balls. Put on a baking sheet with paper on it.
3. After 3 to 5 minutes, the bread should be slightly golden brown. For two to three minutes, turn and cook.
4. In the meantime, put garlic, honey, ketchup, and soy sauce in the middle of the slow cooker. Mix everything together well. Mix the browned meatballs with the sauce slowly.
5. Set the heat to low and let it cook for two to three hours.
6. To serve, top with cilantro and sesame seeds.

66. BEEF CHILI

Prep Time: 15 Minutes | Cook Time: 3 Hour | Total Time: 3 Hour 15 Minutes | Serving: 8

Ingredients

- ✓ 1/2 cup of saltine cracker crumbs
- ✓ 1/4 cup of tomato paste
- ✓ 3 garlic cloves , minced
- ✓ 2 pounds lean ground beef
- ✓ 1 minced jalapeno, optional
- ✓ 1 tsp ground cumin

- ✓ 2 16-ounce cans red kidney beans , rinsed and drained
- ✓ 1 tsp kosher salt
- ✓ 3 tbsp chili powder
- ✓ 29 ounces canned diced tomatoes
- ✓ 1 yellow onion , chopped
- ✓ 1 tsp coarse ground black pepper

Instructions

1. Add the onion and beef to a large pot or cast iron skillet. Bake over medium-high heat until the beef is well browned.
2. Mix it in with the other things in the slow cooker.
3. Put the food in the oven on high for three hours or low for six hours.

67. PORK AND NOODLES

Prep Time: 5 Minutes | Cook Time: 4 Hour 30 Minutes

Total Time: 4 Hour 35 Minutes | Serving: 4

Ingredients

- ✓ Salt and pepper
- ✓ 2 tbsp water
- ✓ 1/2 tsp garlic powder
- ✓ 2 tbsp vegetable oil
- ✓ 1 pork tenderloin (1 1/4 – 1 1/2 pounds)
- ✓ 3/4 cup of water
- ✓ 2 cups of egg noodles uncooked (I use the Amish egg noodles)
- ✓ 1/4 cup of all purpose flour
- ✓ 1/2 tsp onion powder
- ✓ 1 tbsp fresh chopped parsley
- ✓ 2 tbsp Worcestershire sauce
- ✓ 2 tbsp cornstarch
- ✓ 1 can french onion soup (10.5 ounce)

Instructions

1. Put oil in a pan and heat it over medium-low heat. It's time to cook the pork tenderloin. Coat it in flour and then brown it all over in the pan.
2. Put the pork tenderloin that has been browned at the bottom of the slow cooker. Go ahead and add the soup, Worcestershire sauce, garlic powder, and onion powder. Cover and bake for 4 hours at low heat or until the meat is soft. Just before you're done cooking, turn the slow cooker up to high.
3. Mix cornstarch and 2 tbsp of water together to make a smooth paste. Take the pork out of the crock pot and put it on a plate. Mix the cornstarch mixture into the slow cooker. Let it cook and get thicker for 10 minutes with the lid on. Toss the pork with shredded cheese after taking it out of the slow cooker.
4. Put egg noodles and 3/4 cup of water in the slow cooker. Make sure the noodles are submerged in the water. It will take about 30 minutes to cook until the noodles are soft. Wait to cook too long.
5. Add salt and pepper to taste. Serve with fresh parsley that has been chopped on top.

68. CREAMY RANCH CHICKEN RECIPE

Prep Time: 10 Minutes | Cook Time: 8 Hour

Total Time: 8 Hour 10 Minutes | Serving: 6

Ingredients

- ✓ 2 cups of baby carrots
- ✓ 1 cup of milk
- ✓ 1 packet dry ranch dressing mix
- ✓ 1 can cream of chicken soup (10 ounce can)
- ✓ 4 Russet potatoes cut into 2 inch pieces
- ✓ 4 boneless skinless chicken breasts

Instructions

1. Whisk the cream of chicken soup, milk, and ranch dressing together in a small bowl.
2. Fill the crock pot with chicken, potatoes, and carrots. Place these things in the crock pot and pour the sauce on top of them.
3. Set the cooker to low for 6-8 hours or high for 3-4 hours and cover it.
4. Assemble the chicken, potatoes, and carrots. Pour the sauce over them and serve. Enjoy!

69. CHEESY CHICKEN

Prep Time: 20 Minutes | Cook Time: 6 Hour | Total Time: 6 Hour 20 Minutes | Serving: 6

Ingredients

- ✓ 1½ cup of dry stuffing mix
- ✓ 8 pieces Swiss cheese
- ✓ 1 tsp pepper
- ✓ 4 chicken breasts boneless, skinless
- ✓ 1 tsp garlic powder
- ✓ 1 cup of chicken broth
- ✓ 10 ounce Rotel
- ✓ ½ cup of butter melted (1 stick)
- ✓ 1 medium onion chopped
- ✓ 10 ounce cream mushroom soup

Instructions

1. Use a nonstick spray on the crock pot.
2. Put onions in the bottom of the crock pot first, then add the chicken breasts. Put some garlic salt and pepper on top.
3. Add two pieces of Swiss cheese to the top of each chicken breast.
4. Place the chicken on a plate and cover it with melted butter.
5. Add chicken broth and Rotel® and cream of mushroom soup to the chicken.
6. Put the lid on top and cook on low for 8 to 10 hours or high for 6 hours.

70. CHICKEN ENCHILADA CASSEROLE

Prep Time: 5 Minutes | Cook Time: 8 Hour 40 Minutes | Total Time: 8 Hour 45 Minutes | Serving: 8

Ingredients

- ✓ 28 ounce can Red Enchilada Sauce
- ✓ 1.5 pounds boneless skinless raw chicken breasts

Add these items at the end:

- ✓ 3.8 ounce can black olives divided
- ✓ 2 cups of grated cheddar cheese divided
- ✓ 10 corn tortillas

Instructions

1. Combine the chicken breasts and enchilada sauce in a slow cooker.
2. Hide the food for 4 hours or leave it on LOW for 6 to 8 hours.
3. While the chicken is still in the slow cooker, shred it with two forks.
4. Put the tortilla strips in the pan with the chicken and sauce. Stir.
5. Combine half of the olives and 1/2 cup of cheese with the chicken and sauce. Now, stir some more. The mixture should be flattened.
6. The olives and the rest of the cheese should be put on top.
7. For another 40 to 60 minutes, cook on low.
8. Include sour cream on top (not required).

71. EASY CHICKEN CHILI

Prep Time: 15 Minutes | Cook Time: 4 Hours

Total Time: 4 Hours 15 Minutes | Serving: 6

Ingredients

- ✓ 1 tsp smoked paprika
- ✓ 1/2 tbsp ground cumin
- ✓ 1 pound boneless, skinless chicken breasts we used 2 large breasts
- ✓ 15 ounce canned diced tomatoes
- ✓ 1 tbsp minced garlic
- ✓ 12 ounce salsa any kind
- ✓ 15 ounce canned black beans drained and rinsed
- ✓ 1 cup of chicken broth
- ✓ 4 ounce canned diced green chiles
- ✓ 15 ounce canned white northern beans drained and rinsed
- ✓ 2 tsp apple cider vinegar
- ✓ 3 tbsp chili powder

Instructions

1. Put everything into the slow cooker except the chicken breasts. Mix everything together. After that, put chicken breasts on top and cover.
2. Set the crockpot to high and cook for three to four hours or on low for six to eight hours, stirring every now and then.
3. Then, take the chicken out of the crock pot and use two forks to shred it. Combine the shredded chicken back into the crockpot until everything is well-mixed.
4. You can top it with shredded cheese, Greek yogurt, avocado, or anything else you like.

72. SESAME CHICKEN DRUMSTICKS

Prep Time: 5 Minutes | Cook Time: 8 Hours

Total Time: 8 Hours 5 Minutes | Serving: 6

Ingredients

- ✓ 12 chicken drumsticks
- ✓ 3 cloves fresh minced garlic
- ✓ 2 Tbs cornstarch
- ✓ 1 Tbs grated fresh ginger you can use ground ginger, just use a little less
- ✓ sesame seeds for garnishing
- ✓ ¼ cup of honey
- ✓ ½ cup of soy sauce
- ✓ 1½ Tbs toasted sesame oil

Instructions

1. Put the honey, garlic, sesame oil, ginger, and soy sauce in the crock pot and stir them together well. Add the chicken and make sure it's well-covered.
2. Set the timer for 6-8 hours on low or 2-4 hours on high.
3. Take the chicken out of the pan and put the sauce in a small saucepan over medium-low heat.
4. Add equal parts of cold water to the cornstarch and mix well.
5. Mix the slurry with the hot liquid. Boil for one to two minutes or until it gets thick.
6. Put the chicken under the broiler for a few minutes to caramelize after basting it with the sauce. not required)
7. If you want, you can serve it with dipping sauce on the side. Sprinkle with sesame seeds.

73. TURKEY BREAST

Prep Time: 10 Minutes | Cook Time: 4 Hours | Resting time: 10 Minutes

Total Time: 4 Hours 20 Minutes | Serving: 3

Ingredients

For the Turkey:

- ✓ 5 sprigs fresh thyme
- ✓ 1 tbsp Extra virgin olive oil
- ✓ 3 sprigs fresh rosemary
- ✓ 1 tsp sweet paprika
- ✓ 1/2 tbsp salt
- ✓ 1 tsp Onion powder
- ✓ 1 Head of garlic
- ✓ 1 Onion large, yellow or white
- ✓ 1 tsp Dry garlic powder
- ✓ 3 pounds Split turkey breast on the bone
- ✓ Freshly ground pepper

For the gravy:

- ✓ Salt and pepper to taste
- ✓ 1/2 cup of Milk
- ✓ 1-2 tbsp Corn starch
- ✓ 2 cups of Turkey drippings from slow cooker if you have less, add turkey or chicken broth
- ✓ 1 tbsp Lemon Juice (optional)

Instructions

For the Turkey:

1. Separate the garlic cloves in two; Make big pieces of onion;
2. In the bottom of the 6QT slow cooker, put all of these things;
3. On top of the garlic and onion, put the turkey breast.
4. Add the hot sauce, garlic powder, onion powder, paprika, salt, and pepper on top.
5. On top of the turkey, pour extra virgin olive oil;
6. Separate the herbs into bundles and put them in the slow cooker;
7. Once the internal temperature reaches 165F, cover and cook on high for one hour and on low for three hours.Place the skin under the broiler for 3 to 4 minutes to make it extra crispy.

For the Gravy:

1. You can take out the turkey and all the vegetables and herbs when it's done.
2. There will be fat on top of the sauce; take it off so the gravy isn't too heavy. Put the sauce in a small pot.
3. Bring it to boil. Put milk and corn starch in a cup and mix them together.
4. Combine with sauce and cook until it gets thicker.
5. Add salt and pepper if needed after checking the seasoning.
6. Additionally, you can include lemon juice to improve the taste.

74. CHICKEN CORDON BLEU CASSEROLE

Prep Time: 15 Minutes | Cook Time: 5 Hours

Total Time: 5 Hours 15 Minutes | Serving: 6

Ingredients

- ✓ 2 pounds boneless skinless chicken breasts
- ✓ 6 ounce pkg. sliced Swiss cheese
- ✓ ½ tsp pepper
- ✓ ½ tsp garlic powder
- ✓ ½ pound ham slices this doesn't need to exact, just enough slices to cover the chicken
- ✓ ⅓ cup of butter melted
- ✓ 10.5 ounce can cream of chicken soup
- ✓ ½ tsp oregano
- ✓ 6 ounce pkg. cornbread Stove-Top stuffing
- ✓ ¼ cup of milk

Instructions

1. To make the sauce smooth, mix cream of chicken soup, milk, oregano, pepper, and garlic powder in a small bowl. Place away.
2. Spread the chicken breasts out evenly in the slow cooker.
3. Spread out the ham on top of the chicken.
4. Then, add the Swiss cheese in a single layer.
5. Put the soup mix on top, and then use a spatula to spread it out evenly.
6. Put it on top of the cornbread stuffing mix. Spread the butter over the stuffing.
7. For 5 hours, don't open the lid while the food is cooking. Cover and cook on LOW. Serve and have fun!

75. THAI PEANUT CHICKEN

Prep Time: 10 Minutes | Cook Time: 4 Hours

Total Time: 4 Hours 10 Minutes | Serving: 6

Ingredients

- ✓ 1 cup of coconut milk about a half a can
- ✓ 1/3 cup of creamy peanut butter
- ✓ 2 tbsp cornstarch mixed with 2 tbsp water
- ✓ 2 tbsp soy sauce low-sodium
- ✓ 1 tbsp rice wine vinegar
- ✓ 3 garlic cloves minced
- ✓ 1 tbsp ginger peeled and minced
- ✓ 3 chicken breasts boneless and skinless
- ✓ Optional garnishes: chopped peanuts cilantro or green onions
- ✓ 1 tbsp lime juice
- ✓ 2 tbsp honey

Instructions

1. Place the peanut butter, soy sauce, honey, rice wine vinegar, ginger, and garlic in a 6-quart slow cooker. Put the coconut milk and stir until everything is well mixed.
2. Before putting the chicken breasts in the slow cooker, cut them into 1-inch pieces.
3. Set the heat to low and let it cook for four to five hours.
4. Carefully mix the cornstarch and water with the lime juice in the slow cooker.
5. After 20 minutes, cook for another 20 minutes or until the sauce gets thicker.
6. Add any toppings you want, like chopped peanuts, cilantro, green onions, or all three!

76. CHICKEN STEW

Prep Time: 15 Minutes | Cook Time: 8 Hours

Total Time: 8 Hours 15 Minutes | Serving: 12

Ingredients

- ✓ 3 sprigs fresh thyme (or about 1 tsp dried thyme)
- ✓ ½ tsp poultry seasoning
- ✓ 4 medium carrots, peeled and chopped
- ✓ 3 cups of low-sodium chicken broth or chicken stock
- ✓ 2 small cloves garlic, minced or pressed (about 1 tsp)
- ✓ 1 bay leaf
- ✓ 2 medium russet potatoes, peeled and chopped into small bite-sized pieces
- ✓ ½ tsp paprika

For garnish:

- ✓ 1 tbsp cornstarch + 1 tbsp cold water
- ✓ 3 stalks celery, chopped
- ✓ 3-4 pounds bone-in chicken breasts or thighs, skin removed
- ✓ 2 sprigs fresh rosemary (or about 1 tsp dried rosemary)
- ✓ 2 medium sweet onions, chopped into bite-sized pieces
- ✓ chopped fresh parsley
- ✓ Kosher salt and ground black pepper, to taste

Instructions

1. Add potatoes, garlic, bay leaf, 1 tsp of salt, thyme, rosemary, paprika, and poultry seasoning to the bottom of a large slow cooker. Use a stir to mix. Plants and herbs are added to a slow cooker.
2. To taste, put salt and pepper on the chicken. Put the chicken on top of the greens. Chicken breasts with bones on a tray Cover and cook on LOW for 6-8 hours or HIGH for 3-4 hours. Adding chicken broth to the slow cooker.
3. Take the chicken out of the slow cooker about 30 minutes before it's done cooking, and chop or shred the meat. Put the chicken back in the slow cooker and get rid of the bones. If using fresh herbs, throw away the bay leaf and the stems of the herbs.
4. Mix cornstarch and cold water together in a small bowl with a whisk until the mixture is smooth. You can cook the stew on HIGH for 30 minutes without the lid on for 30 minutes or until the broth gets a little thicker. After you taste, you can add more salt and pepper if you'd like. Garnish with chopped fresh parsley right before serving.

77. SLOW-COOKED GOOSE

Prep Time: 20 Minutes | Cook Time: 4 Hour

Total Time: 4 Hour 20 Minutes | Serving: 6

Ingredients

- ✓ 4 tsp canola oil
- ✓ 1/4 cup of butter, cubed
- ✓ 2 tsp Worcestershire sauce
- ✓ 1-1/3 cups of water
- ✓ 1/2 cup of soy sauce
- ✓ 1 envelope onion soup mix
- ✓ 1 can (10-3/4 ounces) condensed golden mushroom soup, undiluted
- ✓ 4 tsp lemon juice
- ✓ Hot cooked mashed potatoes, noodles or rice
- ✓ 3/4 to 1 cup of all-purpose flour
- ✓ 1 tsp garlic powder
- ✓ 2 pounds cubed goose breast

Instructions

1. Put the oil, lemon juice, Worcestershire sauce, garlic powder, and soy sauce in a large, shallow dish. Include goose and coat. Put in the fridge for four hours or overnight.
2. Get rid of the goose and the marinade. In a second large shallow dish, put the flour. Add the goose in pieces and toss to coat. In a big pan set over medium-low heat, brown the goose all over with butter.
3. Put it in a 3-quart slow cooker. Mix the soup mix with water. Cover and cook on high for 4 to 5 hours or until the meat is soft. It goes well with rice, noodles, or potatoes.

78. CRANBERRY TURKEY BREAST

Prep Time: 15 Minutes | Cook Time: 5 Hours

Total Time: 5 Hours 15 Minutes | Serving: 8

Ingredients

- ✓ 1 1-ounce package onion soup mix
- ✓ 2 cups of fresh cranberries enough to cover the bottom of the crock in a single layer
- ✓ ¼ cup of sugar optional for a less cranberry-tart sauce
- ✓ 1 15-ounce can jellied cranberry sauce, sliced into rounds
- ✓ 2 sprigs fresh rosemary optional
- ✓ ½ cup of orange juice
- ✓ 3 to 4 pound boneless turkey breast
- ✓ 2 tbsp butter sliced

Homemade Onion Soup Mix:

- ✓ 2 tbsp bouillon granules beef or chicken both work
- ✓ ¼ tsp celery salt
- ✓ ¼ cup of dried onion flakes
- ✓ ⅛ tsp ground paprika
- ✓ ¼ tsp dried onion powder
- ✓ ⅛ tsp ground black pepper
- ✓ ¼ tsp dried parsley flakes
- ✓ ⅛ tsp dried garlic powder

Instructions

1. Spray cooking spray on a 5 to 6-quart slow cooker to get it ready. Add the whole cranberries and then the sliced cranberry sauce on top. Add HALF of the onion soup mix on top. Put orange juice and sugar (if using) in the crockpot together.
2. To season the turkey, put the turkey breast in the slow cooker and rub it all over with the rest of the onion soup mix. Then, add slices of butter on top of the soup mix. Place the turkey breast next to the rosemary sprigs.
3. Cook: Put the lid on and set the heat to HIGH for an hour. Then turn the heat down to LOW and cook for another 4 to 5 hours, or until the internal temperature reaches 165°F. Before you serve, take out the rosemary sprigs and cut the turkey breast into slices. Mix the cranberry sauce and juices together, then pour them over the turkey.

79. CHICKEN AND STUFFING

Prep Time: 5 Minutes | Cook Time: 5 Hours

Total Time: 5 Hours 5 Minutes | Serving: 4

Ingredients

- 6 ounce box Stove Top chicken stuffing
- 1 cup of (8 ounces) sour cream
- salt and pepper, to taste
- 2 tsp garlic powder, divided use
- 10.5 ounce can cream of chicken soup
- ⅓ cup of water (or milk)
- 10 ounces frozen whole green beans (optional)
- 3 chicken breasts

Instructions

1. Use the crockpot to cook the chicken breasts. Add one tsp of garlic powder, salt, and pepper to chicken breasts to make them taste better.
2. Make a bed of the chicken with the dry Stove Top chicken stuffing mix.
3. A medium-sized bowl should hold cream of chicken soup, sour cream, and water.
4. On top of the stuffing, spread this mixture out.
5. Add the green beans that have been frozen on top. Plus, a little more salt and pepper. Add one tsp of garlic powder again.
6. Place the food in the oven and set it to high for four hours. For chicken to be fully cooked, the temperature inside should reach 165 degrees Fahrenheit.

80. FRENCH ONION CHICKEN

Prep Time: 5 Minutes | Cook Time: 5 Hours

Total Time: 5 Hours 5 Minutes | Serving: 6

Ingredients

- ✓ hot steamed rice
- ✓ ½ cup of water or chicken broth, optional
- ✓ 1 (10.5-ounce) can Unsalted Cream of Chicken Soup
- ✓ 2 (1-ounce) envelopes of Lipton's Onion Soup Mix
- ✓ 3 to 4 boneless skinless chicken breasts

Instructions

1. Put the chicken to the slow cooker and, if you want, season it with salt and pepper.
2. Whisk it in with the soup and soup mix when you add water. Cover the chicken with the sauce. Put the lid on the crock pot and set it to LOW. Cook for 4 to 6 hours.
3. Before you serve, cut the chicken breasts into small pieces. Put it on top of hot steamed rice.

81. CREAM CHEESE CHICKEN

Prep Time: 5 Minutes | Cook Time: 8 Minutes

Total Time: 13 Minutes | Serving: 10

Ingredients

- ✓ 10 ounce Ro-Tel or diced tomatoes
- ✓ 15 ounce canned black beans drained and rinsed
- ✓ 2.5 pounds frozen chicken breast tenderloins
- ✓ 15 ounce can sweet corn drained
- ✓ 8 ounce cream cheese

Instructions

Directions For Slow Cooking:

1. Put everything in your crockpot and set it to low for 6 hours.
2. After 6 hours, take the chicken out of the crock pot.
3. After shredding the chicken, put it back in the crockpot and stir it in to mix it in. Wait 30 to 45 minutes for it to thicken up, then serve.

Directions For Pressure Cooking:

1. Put all the ingredients in. But not the cream cheese to the pot. Then, set the pressure to high and cook for 8 minutes.
2. Before taking off the lid, use Quick Release to let the pressure out of the pot. And. If you want to shred really quickly, you can use a stand mixer.
3. Cut the chicken into small pieces using two forks or your stand mixer.
4. Bring the chicken back to the pot and put the cream cheese. Mix the ingredients together and stir until the cream cheese melts.
5. Put it in the fridge for about 10 to 15 minutes to thicken up. Then serve.

82. COWBOY CASSEROLE

Prep Time: 5 Minutes | Cook Time: 4 Hours

Total Time: 4 Hours 5 Minutes | Serving: 1

Ingredients

- ✓ 1 pound ground beef
- ✓ 1 clove garlic (minced)
- ✓ 15 ounce can diced tomatoes
- ✓ 1 large onion (sliced)
- ✓ 10.5 ounce can cream of chicken soup
- ✓ 1 tsp salt
- ✓ 2 cans kidney beans (do not drain)
- ✓ 1/4 tsp cracked pepper
- ✓ 1/2 tsp dried oregano
- ✓ 1.5 cups of cheddar cheese (grated)
- ✓ 1 tsp italian seasoning
- ✓ 3 large potatoes (sliced)

Instructions

1. Cook the ground beef until it's brown, then drain it well.
2. Put the browned beef and everything else in a crock pot (slow cooker) except the cheese. Mix the ingredients together well.
3. Put the lid on top and cook on high for 4 hours or low for 8 hours.
4. Cover with cheese. Wait about 10 minutes, and then serve when the cheese is melted.

83. CHEESY SPINACH CASSEROLE

Prep Time: 10 Minutes | Cook Time: 5 Hours

Total Time: 5 Hours 10 Minutes | Serving: 8

Ingredients

- ✓ 1/4 cup of flour
- ✓ 2 eggs, beaten
- ✓ 1/2 tsp garlic powder
- ✓ 1/4 cup of butter, cut up
- ✓ 1 1/2 cups of low fat cottage cheese
- ✓ 1 cup of chopped onion
- ✓ 2(16 ounce) bags frozen leaf spinach, thawed, NOT chopped spinach
- ✓ 1/4 - 1/2 tsp salt, to taste
- ✓ 1/4 tsp pepper
- ✓ 2 cups of shredded cheddar cheese
- ✓ 8 ounces low-fat cream cheese, cubed, can use regular

Instructions

1. Use a cooking spray that won't stick on your crock pot.
2. Put everything in the crock pot and mix it well.
3. Cover and cook on low for 4 to 6 hours, or on high for one hour and then on low for two hours. In the middle of cooking, stir. Add one more stir before serving.

84. VEGETABLE CURRY WITH TOFU

Prep Time: 30 Minutes | Cook Time: 4 Hours

Total Time: 4 Hours 30 Minutes | Serving: 4

Ingredients

- ✓ 16 ounce extra firm tofu, drained and pressed
- ✓ 1 small eggplant, chopped
- ✓ 2-3 cups of brown rice or quinoa, for serving (optional)
- ✓ 1 cup of vegetable broth
- ✓ 1 tbsp coconut sugar
- ✓ ¼ cup of Thai green curry paste
- ✓ ¾ cup of peas
- ✓ ½ tsp turmeric
- ✓ 1 medium onion, chopped
- ✓ 1 14.5 ounce can coconut milk
- ✓ 1 tbsp fresh minced ginger
- ✓ 1 tsp salt
- ✓ 1 ½ cups of sliced bell pepper

Instructions

1. Take the tofu out of the package and drain the water. Pull the knobs on the tofu and press tight until the tofu fits well. Put the tofu press on a plate or baking sheet so that the liquid doesn't run off. Tend to the knobs as needed for 30 minutes to an hour as you press. Need a tofu press? Put the tofu between two pieces of paper towels or a kitchen towel. Put it on a plate and cover it with something heavy, like a few books. (Let the tofu press for thirty minutes to an hour.)
2. Add green curry paste, ginger, turmeric, salt, and coconut sugar to the slow cooker. Wait for the tofu to dry out. Mix everything together with a whisk.
3. Mix the eggplant, bell pepper, onion, and peas together by stirring them in. For three to four hours, cook on high.
4. For the next step, spray olive oil spray on a large pan and set it over medium-low heat. Cut the pressed tofu into small pieces that you can easily eat. Remove it from the heat as soon as the tofu turns golden on both sides. After that, put it away.
5. Add the cooked tofu 30 minutes before the curry is done cooking. For the last 30 minutes, let the curry and tofu cook. If you want, you can serve it over brown rice or quinoa.

85. COQ AU VIN

Prep Time: 20 Minutes | Cook Time: 8 Hour

Total Time: 8 Hour 20 Minutes | Serving: 5

Ingredients

- ✓ 2 tbsp butter unsalted
- ✓ 1 bottle Pinot Noir
- ✓ 5 chicken thighs skin on and bone-in
- ✓ 2 tbsp flour
- ✓ 3 garlic cloves minced
- ✓ 3 shallots quartered
- ✓ 1 tsp Kosher salt divided
- ✓ 3 tbsp tomato paste

- ✓ 5 carrots peeled and cut into 1 inch chunks
- ✓ 1/2 tsp coarse ground black pepper
- ✓ 1/2 pound white pearl onions peeled
- ✓ 8 ounces thick-cut bacon diced
- ✓ 1 pound crimini mushrooms halved
- ✓ 2 bay leaves
- ✓ 2 cups of chicken broth
- ✓ 5 fresh thyme sprigs

Instructions

1. Put the bottle of wine in a medium-sized saucepan over high heat. Boil for 15 minutes or until the amount is cut in half.
2. Warm up a cast iron skillet or an aluminum slow cooker insert over high heat. Once the bacon is crispy, take it out of the pan. Add half of the salt and pepper to the chicken.
3. Put them in the pan and brown them on all sides for 4 to 6 minutes or until they are all brown.
4. Take the chicken out of the pan and add the shallots and mushrooms. Then turn down the heat to medium-high. After 3 minutes, stir and cook for another 3 minutes.
5. Put the carrots, mushrooms, shallots, garlic, half of the bacon, broth, the rest of the salt, tomato paste, thyme, bay leaf, pearl onions, and the red wine that has been reduced into a sauce. Put the chicken pieces in the dish and cook on low for 7 hours. Make sure all the ingredients are well mixed.
6. In a small bowl, mix the butter and flour together. After that, put the mixture in the slow cooker and stir it around for another hour or until it gets thicker. Place the rest of the bacon on top and mix it in. Serve.

86. HONEY GARLIC PORK CHOPS

Prep Time: 15 Minutes | Cook Time: 5 Hours | Total Time: 5 Hours 15 Minutes | Serving: 6

Ingredients
- ✓ 6 thick cut boneless pork chops
- ✓ 1/4 cup of honey
- ✓ 2 tbsp cornstarch
- ✓ 1/3 cup of low sodium soy sauce
- ✓ 1/2 cup of ketchup
- ✓ salt and pepper to taste
- ✓ 2 tbsp chopped parsley
- ✓ 1 tbsp olive oil
- ✓ 2 tsp minced garlic

Instructions

1. The oil should be heated in a pan over high heat. Put a lot of salt and pepper on both sides of the pork chops.
2. 4-5 minutes on each side until the pork is a deep golden brown.
3. In the slow cooker, put the pork chops.
4. Combine the garlic, ketchup, soy sauce, and honey in a small bowl. Mix them together using a whisk. Apply the sauce to the pork chops.
5. Set the slow cooker to LOW and cover it. Let it cook for 4 hours.
6. In a small dish, mix 1/4 cup of cold water with cornstarch. On low heat, add the cornstarch mix to the pot.
7. Give it one more hour or until the sauce is just starting to get thick and the pork chops are soft. Add some parsley on top, and serve.

87. GARLIC BUTTER CHICKEN AND VEGGIES

Prep Time: 15 Minutes | Cook Time: 4 Hours | Total Time: 4 Hours 15 Minutes | Serving: 4

Ingredients
- ✓ 1 1/2 pounds Yukon gold potatoes cut into wedges
- ✓ 1 tsp dried parsley
- ✓ 1/2 cup of salted butter melted
- ✓ 1/2 tsp salt
- ✓ 1 tsp. dried thyme leaves
- ✓ 1 1/2 pounds boneless skinless chicken tenders boneless skinless chicken breasts will work fine too
- ✓ 1 Tbsp minced garlic
- ✓ 1 pound bag baby carrots
- ✓ 1/4 tsp pepper

Instructions

1. Put the chicken in the slow cooker in the middle. Put the carrots on one side and the potatoes on the other.
2. Salt, pepper, thyme, and parsley should all be mixed together in a small bowl.
3. Put the butter mix on top of the vegetables and chicken.
4. Put the lid on top and cook on HIGH for 4 hours or low for 6 to 8 hours.
5. Serve and enjoy!

88. HONEY GARLIC CHICKEN

Prep Time: 10 Minutes | Cook Time: 4 Hours

Total Time: 4 Hours 10 Minutes | Serving: 6

Ingredients

- ✓ 5 cloves garlic minced
- ✓ 4 Large bone-in Chicken Breasts skin removed
- ✓ ⅓ cup of honey
- ✓ ⅓ cup of hoisin sauce
- ✓ 1 tsp sesame oil
- ✓ 2 tsp fresh ginger minced
- ✓ ½ cup of low sodium soy sauce
- ✓ 2 tbsp rice vinegar
- ✓ 1 small onion finely diced
- ✓ ¼ tsp red chili flakes
- ✓ 2 tbsp cornstarch

Instructions

1. Put together rice vinegar, sesame oil, fresh ginger, garlic, chopped onion, chili flakes, and honey. Spread sauce over the chicken breasts in the slow cooker. Low-temperature cooking for four to five hours.
2. Grab the chicken from the slow cooker and shred it. Then, set it aside.
3. Add 3 tbsp of water and cornstarch to a small bowl and mix them together. Using a saucepan, bring the liquid from the slow cooker to a boil. Add a little of the cornstarch mixture at a time while stirring the liquid. Keep stirring until it thickens. One minute of boiling.
4. Add sauce to the chicken shreds and mix them together.
5. Place on top of rice and add any toppings you like.

89. CRANBERRY PORK LOIN

Prep Time: 5 Minutes | Cook Time: 6 Hours

Total Time: 6 Hours 5 Minutes | Serving: 8

Ingredients

- ✓ 14 ounce can whole cranberry sauce
- ✓ 4 pound pork loin 3-4 pounds
- ✓ 1 ounce packet Lipton onion soup mix

Optional but recommended for serving:

- ✓ fresh cranberries for garnish
- ✓ 1 can cranberry

Instructions

1. The onion soup mix and cranberry sauce should be mixed together in a small bowl. Pack the pork loin into the crock pot. Pour it over the cranberry mix.
2. Put the lid on top and cook on low for 6 to 7 hours. Do not open the lid during that time. Slow-cooked sauce goes well with the sliced meat.

90. BEEF ROAST WITH GINGER SNAP GRAVY

Prep Time: 15 Minutes | Cook Time: 4 Hours

Total Time: 4 Hours 15 Minutes | Serving: 8

Ingredients

- ✓ 3 large potatoes peeled and cut in chunks
- ✓ 2 cloves garlic minced
- ✓ 3 cups of beef stock
- ✓ 6 carrots peeled and cut in chunks
- ✓ Pam to spray the pot
- ✓ 1 medium onion peeled and cut in chunks
- ✓ 6 stalks of celery cut in chunks
- ✓ 1 small chuck roast 2 pounds
- ✓ ¼ tsp black pepper
- ✓ 2 tbsp fresh ginger peeled and grated
- ✓ 2 tbsp olive oil
- ✓ 8 gluten free ginger snap cookies

Instructions

Meat & Vegetables Directions:

1. Put the olive oil in a big pan and heat it up. On both sides, brown the meat a little. Spray Pam cooking spray on a 6-quart crockpot.
2. Put the meat in the crock pot.
3. In a frying pan, bake the onion until it is clear and starts to turn a little brown. Put in the carrots and brown them a bit.
4. Put the potatoes, onions, carrots, celery, and spices in the crockpot.
5. Put in the beef stock. First, cook on high for an hour. Then lower the heat to low and cook for three hours.
6. Food and meat should be taken out of the broth. While you make the gravy, put them in a warm oven to keep them hot.

Gravy Directions:

1. Put the broth in a pot.
2. Take the ginger cookies and crush them (I used a small food processor). Then, add them to the broth. On medium-high heat, cook until it gets thick. To taste, add salt and pepper. Serve right away with meat and vegetables.

91. HOT CHOCOLATE

Prep Time: 5 Minutes | Cook Time: 2 Hours

Total Time: 2 Hours 5 Minutes | Serving: 12

Ingredients

- ✓ 14 ounce can sweetened condensed milk
- ✓ 2 cups of semi-sweet chocolate chips
- ✓ 2 tsp pure vanilla extract
- ✓ ¼ cup of unsweetened cocoa powder
- ✓ mini marshmallows, for serving
- ✓ 2 cups of heavy whipping cream
- ✓ 6 cups of whole milk, divided use

Instructions

1. Put one cup of milk in a bowl or cup of that can go in the microwave. Heat it until it's steaming but not boiling. You can do this on the stove in a small saucepan as well.
2. Mix the 1/4 cup of cocoa powder into the milk slowly with a whisk.
3. Put the sweetened condensed milk, whole milk, heavy whipping cream, vanilla extract, and semisweet chocolate chips in a slow cooker that holds 4 quarts or more. Last, add the cocoa and milk mix that you made earlier.
4. Put the lid on top and cook on low for about two hours. As it starts to warm up, stir it around a lot. It's very important to stir the chocolate chips into the rest of the mixture so that they melt evenly. You want to avoid a big chocolate mess on the bottom.
5. As soon as all the chocolate chips melt and the mixture gets warm, it's done.
6. Put it in mugs and add marshmallows, whipped cream, and a small candy cane on top.

92. CARAMEL DIP

Prep Time: 5 Minutes | Cook Time: 1 Hours

Total Time: 1 Hours 5 Minutes | Serving: 96

Ingredients

- ✓ 2 cans sweetened condensed milk
- ✓ 2 cups of brown sugar (packed)
- ✓ 1 cup of unsalted butter
- ✓ 1 cup of light corn syrup

Instructions

1. Put the butter in a 4-quart crock pot and melt it on high.
2. Put in the brown sugar and mix it in with a whisk until the melted butter is fully mixed in.
3. Put the corn syrup and sweetened condensed milk in the crock pot and stir them together until they are well mixed.
4. Keep the heat on low for an hour and stir it every now and then until it thickens.
5. When it gets thick, either turn off the crock pot or set it to warm. Serve it right from the slow cooker or move it to a bowl for serving.
6. Apple slices, pretzels, graham cracker cookies, strawberries, or banana slices should go with it. Put any extra caramel in a container with a lid and put it in the fridge.
7. This recipe makes a quart of caramel dip.

93. SLOW-COOKED RICE PUDDING

Prep Time: 5 Minutes | Cook Time: 2 Hours

Total Time: 2 Hours 5 Minutes | Serving: 6

Ingredients

- ✓ 1 cup of (250 ml) 35% cream
- ✓ 1 tsp (5 ml) vanilla extract
- ✓ 1 cup of (250 ml) arborio or other short-grain rice
- ✓ 1 pinch salt
- ✓ 4 cups of (1 litre) milk
- ✓ 1/2 cup of (125 ml) sugar

Instructions

1. Put the rice, cream, milk, and salt in the slow cooker. Put the lid on top and cook on high for two hours. Mix the vanilla and sugar together until the sugar is gone. You can serve it hot or cold. Let some of it cool down. Serve hot or cover and put in the fridge.

94. BANANA BREAD

Prep Time: 10 Minutes | Cook Time: 3 Hours

Total Time: 3 Hours 10 Minutes | Serving: 8

Ingredients

- ✓ 1 tsp baking powder
- ✓ 1/4 cup of cinnamon chips
- ✓ 1/2 tsp baking soda
- ✓ 2 cups of flour
- ✓ 1 stick butter
- ✓ 1 tsp vanilla
- ✓ 1 cup of sugar
- ✓ 3 bananas, overripe
- ✓ 2 eggs
- ✓ 1/2 tsp cinnamon

Instructions

1. Come together and mix all the wet things. You can do this first if you want to. It was all put into my small stand mixer.
2. Add all the dry ingredients and mix them together.
3. Mix the dry ingredients into the wet ones until everything is well mixed.
4. Add the chips and mix them in. Feel free to make the amount bigger.
5. Put baking spray on your slow cooker and then add the mix. I sprayed out a lot of air when I ran out of baking spray. That's another reason why my edges burned.
6. Put a paper towel under the lid to soak up any extra water. Take off the paper towel for the last half hour of cooking. Set the timer for two hours on high.

95. OATMEAL RAISIN COOKIE OVERNIGHT OATS

Prep Time: 5 Minutes | Cook Time: 8 Hours

Total Time: 8 Hours 5 Minutes | Serving: 6

Ingredients

- ✓ 1 cup of long-cooking steel-cut oats uncooked
- ✓ 2 cups of whole milk
- ✓ 1 tsp cinnamon
- ✓ 1/2 cup of raisins
- ✓ 1 tsp vanilla
- ✓ 1/4 cup of sugar
- ✓ 3/4 cup of brown sugar packed
- ✓ 2 tbsp butter melted
- ✓ 1/4 tsp salt
- ✓ Optional garnish: additional milk

Instructions

1. Lightly coat a bowl that will fit in your crock pot with cooking spray.
2. Put everything into a bowl and mix it well.
3. Put your bowl in the crock pot. The large bowl from this set works best. Pour water into the crock pot, not into the bowl, until it's halfway up the bowl. Do not put water halfway up the bowl's side, or the water could get into the oats.
4. Set the temperature to low and cover the pot.

96. RED VELVET BREAD PUDDING

Prep Time: 5 Minutes | Cook Time: 3 Hours

Total Time: 3 Hours 5 Minutes | Serving: 8

Ingredients

- ✓ 1/2 cup of white chocolate chips
- ✓ Cream Cheese Frosting if desired
- ✓ 3 eggs
- ✓ 6 cups of red velvet cake unfrosted, cut into cubes
- ✓ 1/2 tsp vanilla
- ✓ 1 1/2 cups of milk or cream
- ✓ 1/4 cup of sugar

Instructions

1. Add cake cubes to your crock pot.
2. Mix the milk, vanilla, eggs, and sugar in a different bowl using a whisk. Spread the mix on top of the red velvet cake. Put the white chocolate chips and stir them in a little. Put it on high for two to three hours.
3. You can drizzle it with cream cheese frosting, but you can also eat it plain!
4. Be careful, this makes a lot, so get some friends over!

97. WHITE CHEESE DIP

Prep Time: 10 Minutes | Cook Time: 30 Minutes

Total Time: 40 Minutes | Serving: 5

Ingredients

- ✓ 1/2 tsp garlic salt
- ✓ (1) 4.5 ounce can of diced green chilies (do not drain)
- ✓ 1 pound white American Cheese chopped into smaller pieces
- ✓ 1/2 tsp cumin
- ✓ 1/2 cup of milk

Instructions

1. Put the chopped White American Cheese in a 1.5-quart crock pot.
2. After that, add the milk, green chilies, and spices.
3. Stir. Cover and cook on low heat until melted, stirring every now and then.
4. Is the cheese sauce too thick? Just add more milk when it's time to serve.

98. LEMON CURD

Prep Time: 20 Minutes | Cook Time: 6 Hours

Total Time: 6 Hours 20 Minutes | Serving: 2

Ingredients

- ✓ 4 eggs
- ✓ 125g unsalted butter
- ✓ 1 orange
- ✓ 400g caster sugar (most of a small packet)
- ✓ 3 lemons

Instructions

1. Get the fruit's juice and zest. If you don't have a zesting tool, you can grate the peels.
2. Put the sugar, juice, and zest in a saucepan with the butter. Stir the mixture slowly over low heat until the sugar and butter melt.
3. Put the mix in the bowl or basin and let it cool for 10 minutes. Whip the eggs while it cools down. Mixing the eggs well after adding them to the other things is important.
4. Cover the bowl with tin foil. It takes to add enough hot water to the slow cooker to cover the sides of the bowl by half. Put the lid on top of the slow cooker.
5. For four to six hours, on the low setting, until the curd is cooked and thick. Every two hours, give it a quick stir.
6. Clean out your jars. Put hot lemon curd in them and let them cool.

99. ROCKY ROAD CHOCOLATE CAKE

Prep Time: 15 Minutes | Cook Time: 4 Hours

Total Time: 4 Hours 15 Minutes | Serving: 8-10

Ingredients

- ✓ 1 (4 ounce) package instant chocolate pudding mix
- ✓ 1/2 cup chopped pecans
- ✓ 1 cup semisweet chocolate morsel
- ✓ 1/3 cup butter, melted
- ✓ 1 cup sour cream
- ✓ 3 1/4 cups milk, divided
- ✓ 1 (3 1/2 ounce) package chocolate cook-and-serve pudding mix
- ✓ 1 (18 1/4 ounce) package German chocolate cake mix
- ✓ 3 large eggs, lightly beaten
- ✓ 1 teaspoon vanilla extract
- ✓ 1 1/2 cups miniature marshmallows
- ✓ vanilla ice cream (optional)

Instructions

1. Applying an electric mixer, mix the cake mix, the next five ingredients, and 1 1/4 cups of milk for two minutes on medium speed. When you need to, stop the mixer and scrape down the sides. A 4-quart slow cooker that has been lightly greased should be used to put the batter in.
2. In a heavy nonaluminum saucepan, cook the last 2 cups of milk over medium heat, stirring often, for 3-5 minutes or until bubbles form (do not boil). Take the saucepan off the heat.
3. Add cook-and-serve pudding mix on top of the batter. Very slowly, pour hot milk over the pudding. Set the temperature to LOW and cover the pan.
4. Toast the pecans in a small nonstick skillet over medium-low heat for three to five minutes, stirring them around a lot until they start to smell good.
5. Leave the slow cooker off. Give the cake some pecans, marshmallows, and chocolate morsels to sprinkle on top. Wait 15 minutes, or until the marshmallows start to melt a bit.
6. Put it in dessert dishes and, if you want, serve it with ice cream.

100. REESE'S PEANUT BUTTER CUP CHOCOLATE CAKE

Prep Time: 15 Minutes | Cook Time: 2 Hours

Total Time: 2 Hours 15 Minutes | Serving: 10

Ingredients

- ✓ 8 ounce pkg. mini Reese's peanut butter cups
- ✓ 1 cup of water
- ✓ 15.25 ounce devil's food cake mix
- ✓ 1/2 cup of salted butter melted
- ✓ 3 large eggs

For the topping:

- ✓ 1 cup of creamy peanut butter
- ✓ 10 bite size Reese's peanut butter cups
- ✓ 3 Tbsp powdered sugar

Slow Cooker Size:

- ✓ 6 quart oval

Instructions

1. Combine the cake stir, water, butter, and eggs in a large bowl. Mix the ingredients completely. Not worrying about the lumps, that's normal. Drops of peanut butter should be mixed in.
2. Cover the slow cooker with nonstick spray. Cover the slow cooker with foil and pour the batter into it. Spread it out evenly.
3. Place the lid on top and cook on HIGH for two hours. Do not open the lid during that time.
4. When the time is up, take the cake off the heat so it no longer cooks.
5. The peanut butter should be put in a small pan that is set over medium heating on the stove. Watch closely because it will burn quickly as you stir it until it melts and becomes smooth. Combine the powdered sugar with the mixture and mix it well using a whisk.
6. Spread the sweetened peanut butter on top of the hot cake. Cover with Reese's peanut butter cups of that have been cut in half.
7. Assemble and enjoy! Delicious with whipped cream or ice cream.

65780809R00057